*Camille Glenn's*

# OLD-FASHIONED
# CHRISTMAS
# COOKBOOK

# ALSO BY CAMILLE GLENN

THE HERITAGE OF SOUTHERN COOKING

A SPECIAL COLLECTION OF SALADS, SOUPS AND STEWS

THE FINE ART OF DELECTABLE DESSERTS

*Camille Glenn's*

# OLD-FASHIONED
# CHRISTMAS
# COOKBOOK

ALGONQUIN BOOKS OF CHAPEL HILL 1996

Published by

ALGONQUIN BOOKS OF CHAPEL HILL

Post Office Box 2225

Chapel Hill, North Carolina 27515-2225

a division of

WORKMAN PUBLISHING

708 Broadway

New York, New York 10003

LIBRARY OF CONGRESS CATALOGING-IN-PUBLICATION DATA

Glenn, Camille.

Camille Glenn's old-fashioned Christmas cookbook / Camille Glenn.

p.   cm.

Includes index.

ISBN 1-56512-120-1

1. Christmas cookery.   2. Cookery, American—Southern style.

3. Menus.   I. Title.

TX739.2.C45G54   1996

641.5'68—dc20   96-9194

CIP

10  9  8  7  6  5  4  3  2  1

First Edition

*To Suzanne Rafer, Ruth Chaffins,*
*Barbara Winter, and Ruth Bos,*
*without whose loyalty and help this book*
*never could have gone to press.*

The art of cooking is a universal feature
of civilized and cultural life, and
we must do our best to preserve it.

–Camille Glenn

# CONTENTS

MENU 6 54

Champagne or Chilled White Wine

*Brie and Red Bell Pepper Pie*

Italian Bread

*Bibb, Endive, Artichoke, and
Prosciutto Salad*

*Bartlett Pear and Pineapple Sherbet*

*White Christmas Truffles*

Demitasse

## CHRISTMAS MORNING BREAKFAST

MENU 7 62

Fruit Juice

Broiled Bacon or Sausage

*Old-Fashioned Buttermilk Waffles
with Tangerine Syrup*

*German Apple Pancakes*

*Wonderful Cranberry Preserves*

Black Bing Cherry Preserves

*Very Special French Toast with
Cinnamon and Coriander Mélange*

Coffee, Tea

## A HEARTY HOLIDAY BREAKFAST OR SUPPER

MENU 8 75

*Corned Beef Hash with Creamy Hot
Mustard or Lorenzo Sauce*

Poached Eggs

*Cottage Cheese Yeast Biscuits*

*Especially Delicious Pear Preserves*

Fruit in Season

Coffee

## CHRISTMAS DAY DINNERS

MENU 9 84

Champagne

Caviar on Toast Points

*Roast Suckling Pig*

*Roast Turkey Breast Lined with
Country Ham*

*Spiced Moro Oranges*

*Spiced Walnuts on Watercress*

*Shredded Brussels Sprouts*

*Four-Star Cornmeal
Butterflake Biscuits*

*Kentucky Eggnog Ice Cream*

*Mother's Ambrosia*

*Plum Pudding Pie*

*Chocolate Almond Toffee*

Demitasse

## AN ELEGANT CHRISTMAS DINNER

## A FIRESIDE HOLIDAY PICNIC

MENU 13   136

*Smoked Breast of Chicken
with Prunes*

*Ham in Rosemary Buns*

*Egg Salad Sandwiches with
Capers and Tarragon*

*Classic English Fruitcake*

*Kentucky Bourbon Fruitcake Cookies*

*A Favorite Deep-South Pecan Cookie*

*Fabulous Chocolate Marionettes*

*Luscious Apricot-Orange Candy*

*St. Augustine Mincemeat Cookies*

*New Orleans Eggnog*

*Biscuit Tortoni*

Coffee

## A CHRISTMAS LUNCHEON

MENU 15   172

Chilled White Wine

*My Favorite Shrimp Salad*

Rosemary Buns or French Baguettes

*Chocolate Pots-de-Crème*

*Tiny Banana Muffins or
Dainty Pecan Muffins*

*Williamsburg Bourbon Truffles*

Coffee

## A CHRISTMAS TEA PARTY

MENU 14   154

*Tea Party Sandwiches:
Sandwich Rolls, Ribbon Sandwiches,
Pinwheel Sandwiches, and
Sandwich Loaves*

*Hazelnut Marionettes, Almond
Contessas, Marvelous Gingersnaps,
Mincemeat Turnovers, Kathy's
Dried Cherry Scones, and Ginger
Roll with Marrons*

*The Chartwell Cake*

Tea

## MENUS FOR RINGING IN
## THE NEW YEAR

MENU 16   180

Champagne, Chilled White Wine

*Creole Shrimp with Rice*

*Bibb Lettuce Salad with Dijon
Vinaigrette Dressing*

French Bread

*New Orleans Madeleines*

*Light Opera Soufflé*

Coffee

# WITH APPRECIATION

At my age, many of my closest friends and loved ones have gone on before me, but I wish to thank those who are still with me for their encouragement and thoughtfulness to me through the years: Allie Carr, Mary Drummond, Col. and Mrs. Henry G. Hamby, Orton Hamby, Jan Applegate, Dr. Forrest and Mary Julia Kuhn, Dr. Lynn Speevac and staff, Dr. A. Franklin White, Molly Johnson, Mark and Betty Senter, Mr. and Mrs. Tom Baker, Mike Kephart, Deborah Ford, Tony Lindauer, Dee Rushing, Peggy Harvin, Richard Grausman, Harriet Robbins, Catherine Greenwell, Ruth Murphy, Sandy Pike, Larry and Connie Brodt, Peter Workman, Don and Ruth Miller, Joe and Kathleen Castro, Elaine Buckley, Mary Walter, Judy Chapman, Kay Gill, Jack Kersey, Dr. Charles Gruenberger, Bob Smith, Bob and Margaret Kulp, Mark and Susie Stevens, Vivian Beard, Betty Taylor, Sarah Fritschner, Wade Hall, Mr. and Mrs. Steve Tipton, Bill and Jane Woolsey, Dr. Edward and Gloria Shrader, Dan Maye, Dr. Clinton Cook, Philip Cooke, Will and Kathy Cary, Carol Greene, Mrs. C. K. McClure, Scott and Robin Hansel, Pat Cross, Alice Colombo, Dr. William Peak and Patsie, Cindy Inskeep, Arlene Jacobsen, Memsy Price, Dr. Mark and Hedvika Heinicke, and Bob Holmes.

And most of all, I wish to thank my children, Camille G. Perry and Elissa Glenn.

# INTRODUCTION

I was born when the twentieth century was nine years old, going on ten, just in time for the Christmas baking and preserving to get under way. Naturally I do not remember that first Christmas, but it was my introduction to a world perfumed with cinnamon, cloves, ginger, and allspice simmering in kettles of mincemeat and other sweet things for the holidays. I did not choose my fate, but I must have loved it because I have been in the midst of it ever since, without the slightest wish to escape.

I believe there is a certain depth and beauty in a home, no matter how humble, when there is grace and love in a kitchen that is alive with the warmth of good things cooking for our families and friends to eat.

To wait for the luxuries—or to postpone quiet pleasures that are at hand, in the race that is propelled by fashion—is to miss a part of life that is meaningful.

When the summer visitors had gone, our little town was very quiet in the winter, even at Christmas, except for the jingle of bells, the decorating of Christmas trees, and the secret but silent competition in the kitchens over who baked the best cakes, candies, and holiday pies in town! Such covert action seems strange to us now—that such a commotion would be made over such simple things—but the holiday treats could not be bought in those days and, anyway, they were the homemakers' creative outlet.

I have never failed to believe that good food is life-enhancing. The menus for our Christmas celebrations, to be successful, must be in keeping with the season and in harmony with the occasion. The flavors must blend in counterpoint, just as in music. Then and only then can we be assured that, as Henri Faugeron (the Parisian restaurateur) said, "In cooking, as in every human endeavor, all *can* be art."

So, to his majesty the suckling pig, to the Southern country ham that has no superior, to the turkey and all the trimmings, the winter vegetables, the bourbon-scented cakes of old, and the pies and gingerbread—we salute you, with gratefulness in our hearts and a Merry Christmas to all!

Christmas is such a special time to the entire Christian world, it seems fitting to me to refresh our memories and our thoughts concerning the depth of meaning that has sustained the commemoration of this holiday.

The heritage of Christmas goes back to the most ancient of times, but from its inception it has been an ambivalent mixture of religion and festivities. The first celebrations of the Christian faith were based upon the drama of the pagan worship of the sun, the winter solstice it was called—the deep dark of night that gave way to the glimmer of light that came with the dawn. It is difficult for us to imagine the depth of darkness in the world before candles, whale oil or kerosene lamps, and, later, electricity. The return of the sun was the only light for these people.

The bonfires, the burning of the logs, and the candlelight of the festivals dedicated to the Roman god Saturn for the return of the sun were transposed to give meaning to Christ's birth as the "Light of the World." The grafting of a new faith upon old beliefs through the millennia has left indelible traces of influence upon the framework of our convictions. In that vein, the vibrancy of the Roman feasts and carnivals that antedated Christianity has drifted down through the ages so imperceptibly that few have been aware of the origin of the inherited spirit of the revelries.

The word *Christmas* (literally Christ's mass), as well as many of our present customs, such as decorating the evergreen tree with lights and colorful objects, came to us directly from Germany and England, and it was from the Victorian era in these two countries that our patterns of Yuletide celebration evolved.

Following the ritual custom of his native Germany, Prince Albert, Queen Victoria's consort, in 1840 had a huge tree (called a *Tannenbaum* in German) decked with candles and set aglow in Buckingham Palace. This was the first Christmas tree of renown, and the tradition passed rather quickly down to us in the former colonies.

In the early days of our country, the Puritans in New England frowned upon the frivolity of Christmas, but in the South it was a different story. The South possessed a culinary wealth of rich farmlands, abundant game, fish, and seafood, as well as a warm and comforting climate. The Southern colonizers—the English in Virginia and the Carolinas, the French in Louisiana, the Spanish in Florida and Alabama, and the Germans in Kentucky and the Ohio valley—nurtured the celebration of Christmas from the beginning. It was a period of rest for the farmhands and was greeted as a happy time for all. The winters were not as harsh then and the provisions were bountiful. Old World caroling was revived, as well as the Yule log, the garlanded tree, lush greenery, and decorations. And, may I add, wonderful food was the first priority, and it has remained an integral part of our temperament to this day. It is said that we have a hospitable nature, and I believe we do. This spirit is conducive to Christmas being a happy time, just as it should be.

This cookbook is laden with nostalgia of Christmas past and the memories of delicious foods that were cooked in the South, by my family and by me. For my part, they cover a period of more than sixty years. Time changes many things, fashions come and go, but the good remains. This I believe, and I have written this book for you with that in mind.

# Tree-Trimming Parties

## Menu 1

*Chili Pot Roast with Green Chili Tomato Sauce*
*Red Cabbage and Parsley Slaw*
French Bread
*Country Squire Cookies*
*Sugarplum Cookies*
*Ginger and Marmalade Pudding*
Coffee

One of the most hectic but fun things we do at Christmas is trim the tree. Each and every family member is a self-appointed decorator and wants to supervise. Haven't you noticed?

In the country, when I was young, we had to go into the woods to select a tree. It would take ages to decide the size, shape, and how it would fit into the house. Then the strongest one, the one who could handle the saw, cut down the tree. These days we go to the markets that have Christmas trees by the hundreds, all cut and ready to go. I believe going into the pine groves to find a tree was more fun, but those days are gone.

The ornaments, angels, silver and gold tinsel ribbons, and music boxes that would play "Silent Night" were stored in the attic after each Christmas, multiplying each year until we had quite an eclectic selection to choose from. The limbs of the tree could barely hold the entire collection.

The most beautiful Christmas tree I have ever seen was one designed by my best friend, the late Frankie Sams. (My children called her Aunt Frankie, so most of us adults did, too.) Frankie was a professional floral designer and she had no peer. One Christmas she found some woven silk birds and ornaments made by a company in Florence, Italy, from which she often bought inimitable silk flowers.

We called it the Peacock Tree. The tree was very large and bespangled as if it were alive with small woven silk peacocks in lustrous blues and greens, with dashes of silver and golden thread and tiny touches of black centers, the exact replicas of real peacocks. There were also small silk turtledoves in a soft yellow, and many round balls woven of the same translucent silk colors to match the birds that hung by their sides. Several larger peacocks were tucked in the folds of green velvet at the foot of the tree, strutting around in their elegant and dramatic presence, spreading their wings in all their reverberant glory, as if to say, "Am I not beautiful?"

There were, of course, strings of tiny electric lights all in the same soft yellow that sparkled like hundreds of diamonds hanging in garlands on the tree.

The children's tree was in the family room, and that is where the presents were kept, to be unwrapped on Christmas morning. The peacocks and turtledoves that represented the twelve days of Christmas were in the living room.

We spent many Christmases with Frankie, but that one remains the most vivid in my memory.

I have planned the tree-trimming menus as best I could with dishes that can be cooked ahead, but some things, to be delicious, must be done at the last minute.

To be really wonderful, food must be made of the freshest and highest-quality ingredients. Christmas comes but once a year and it is supposed to be the merriest time—let's make it so—and very beautiful, just like Aunt Frankie's peacocks.

## CHILI POT ROAST WITH GREEN CHILI TOMATO SAUCE

Spain was the first European nation to lay claim to the territory we now know as the state of Alabama. The Spaniards landed at Mobile Bay in 1507 and since they had come straight from Mexico, they brought their chili peppers with them.

Those chili peppers were found to have a natural affinity for the rich ocean-misted soil around the bay, and the scattered few but friendly people in the area had a seemingly natural palate for the sting and heat of the peppers.

Spicy seasonings are still popular in the Deep South, especially in Alabama, where the inhabitants are proud of their inherited Spanish ways—and their peppers.

This Chili Pot Roast is perfect for the fun and informality of decorating the Christmas tree. The roast can be prepared a day or two ahead, refrigerated, and reheated, if you like (in fact, the flavor will improve). It can be served warm, carved into slices, with hominy, grits, or potatoes. Or, if you choose, the slices can be served on sesame buns or in pita pockets along with a salad of various lettuces or shredded cabbage.

4½ to 5 pounds beef rump or brisket
1½ tablespoons vegetable oil, olive oil, or beef drippings
Salt to taste
1 cup homemade beef or veal stock
4 medium onions, peeled and diced
2 imported bay leaves
3 tablespoons chili powder, or to taste
1 cup Green Chili Tomato Sauce (recipe follows)
1 teaspoon dried basil or oregano
Tabasco sauce to taste
Sprigs of fresh watercress, cilantro, or parsley,
    for garnish

1. Preheat the oven to 450°F.
2. Brush the roast on all sides with the oil (this will help it brown evenly) and season it with salt.
3. Place the roast in a large, shallow baking pan. Set it on the lower rack of the preheated oven and allow it to brown, about 30 minutes.
4. Remove the roast from the oven and reduce the heat to 325°F. Transfer the roast to a deeper casserole or roaster that has a cover. Add the browned bits and drippings from the baking pan.
5. Add the stock, onions, and bay leaves. Sprinkle the roast with the chili powder.
6. Cover the casserole or roaster, return it to the oven, and cook the meat for about 30 minutes, basting frequently.
7. Add the Green Chili Tomato Sauce, basil, and Tabasco. Taste and add salt if needed. Cover the roast again and continue to cook, basting every 30 minutes or so, until it is very tender, about 2 more hours. If the sauce becomes overly thick at any time, add more Green Chili Tomato Sauce or stock.

8.  When the roast is tender, transfer it to a carving board. Skim the excess fat from the sauce in the pan and discard the bay leaves. Slice the roast and arrange it on a warm platter. Pour the sauce over the meat and garnish with watercress.

Serves 10 to 12

# GREEN CHILI TOMATO SAUCE

This recipe makes more than enough sauce for the pot roast. You can pass the extra in a sauceboat or refrigerate it to use with another meal. It's especially good with sandwiches made of leftover roast or meat loaf.

1 large can (35 ounces) imported plum tomatoes (good-quality
    Italian tomatoes are best)
3 tablespoons extra-virgin olive oil
⅓ cup chopped onion
1 clove garlic, whole and unpeeled (optional)
2 to 3 tablespoons chopped canned green chilies
2 tablespoons chopped fresh basil leaves, or 1½ teaspoons dried basil
Salt to taste

1.  Purée the tomatoes, with their juice, in a blender or food processor. Pour the purée into a heavy saucepan.
2.  Add the olive oil, onion, and garlic and cook until the mixture has thickened. Discard the garlic.
3.  Add the green chilies and basil. Salt to taste. Cook for about 2 minutes. Taste and correct the seasoning if necessary.

When garlic cloves are left whole and cooked unpeeled, the flavor they give to the dish is much milder than when they're peeled and chopped.

## RED CABBAGE AND PARSLEY SLAW

One of the best slaws in the whole world. It's especially good with pot roasts, tender steaks, fried or broiled chicken, loin of pork, veal chops, or a veal roast.

*½ small head red cabbage*
*2 cups chopped fresh parsley*
*Classic Vinaigrette Dressing (recipe follows)*

Shred the cabbage exceedingly fine by hand or in a food processor. You should have about 2 cups. Add the parsley. Transfer to a serving bowl and toss with the Classic Vinaigrette Dressing.

Serves 4

VARIATION:
You may substitute radicchio for the cabbage.

 The cabbage must be tender and crisp.

## CLASSIC VINAIGRETTE DRESSING

*1 tablespoon white or red wine vinegar*
*1 tablespoon salt*
*4 tablespoons extra-virgin olive oil*
*Fresh lemon juice to taste (optional)*

1.   Combine the vinegar and salt. Mix well.
2.   Add the olive oil and blend until well mixed. Add lemon juice to taste.

Makes about ¼ cup

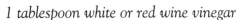

The proportions are a straightforward 1-to-4 ratio (vinegar/salt to oil). You may increase this recipe, using the same proportions, by as much as you like.

The lemon juice is not essential, but it adds a delightful touch of freshness.

Never use malt vinegar! Wine vinegar makes a far superior vinaigrette.

## COUNTRY SQUIRE COOKIES

This is one of the most delightful—and easiest—Christmas cookies I know. It lends itself to many variations—it can be made by hand, quite plain, or put through a cookie press if that is your wish. It is a merry Christmas addition to a cup of tea.

*1 cup (2 sticks) unsalted butter, at room temperature, but not overly soft*
*1 cup sugar, or ¼ cup light brown sugar and ¾ cup granulated sugar*
*3 large egg yolks*
*2½ cups sifted all-purpose flour*
*2 teaspoons baking powder*
*½ teaspoon salt*
*1½ teaspoons cognac vanilla (see page 29) or 1 tablespoon cognac*
*3 tablespoons chopped unsalted pistachios or pecans (optional)*

1.  Preheat the oven to 350°F.
2.  Cream the butter and sugar with an electric mixer or in a food processor. (The mixer makes a more delicate and less compact cookie.)
3.  Add the egg yolks and beat until the mixture looks like mayonnaise.
4.  Sift the flour with the baking powder and salt and mix in quickly. Do not overbeat.
5.  Add the cognac vanilla. Mix in the nuts by hand if you are using them. Transfer the dough to a bowl, cover, and chill in the refrigerator until firm enough to roll out easily, about 1 hour.

6.  Form the chilled dough into balls, about a generous tablespoon each for a dainty cookie. Place them about 1½ inches apart on a nonstick or lightly greased pastry sheet. Flatten them a bit with your fingers or the bottom of a water glass.
7.  Place the pastry sheet on the middle rack of the preheated oven and bake until the cookies are a very delicate brown, 10 to 12 minutes.

Makes about 3 dozen cookies

VARIATIONS:

*New Orleans Praline Cookies:* Use 1 cup light brown sugar and ½ cup coarsely chopped pecans. For real New Orleans flavor, add 2 teaspoons praline liqueur and reduce the cognac vanilla to 1 teaspoon.

*Turbinado Cookies:* Reduce the sugar to ¾ cup. Roll the dough balls in turbinado (raw) sugar and bake as directed.

## SUGARPLUM COOKIES

This is a flavorful holiday cookie full of spices and apricots and almonds. The cookies can be made ahead, as they keep well.

Zest of 1 navel orange
Zest of ½ lemon
1 cup sugar
1 cup (2 sticks) unsalted butter, at room temperature
2 large eggs
1½ cups sifted all-purpose flour
1½ teaspoons baking powder
½ teaspoon salt
1 teaspoon ground cinnamon
1 teaspoon ground allspice
⅛ teaspoon ground cloves
⅛ teaspoon ground coriander
1½ cups dried apricots, cut into thirds and slightly softened in enough
     boiling orange juice almost to cover
1½ cups chopped almonds
1½ teaspoons Cointreau or cognac
Cookie Glaze (optional; recipe follows)

1.  Preheat the oven to 350°F.
2.  Grate the orange and lemon zest by hand, or combine the zest with the sugar in a food processor and twirl until the zest is finely grated.
3.  Add the sugar (if not already combined with the zest) and butter and beat until creamy. Add the eggs and beat thoroughly.
4.  Sift the flour with the baking powder, salt, and spices and add to the egg mixture.
5.  Fold in the apricots (with the orange juice), almonds, and Cointreau by hand.

Have you ever heard
 of the Sugarplum
 Tree?
'Tis a marvel of great
 renown!
It blooms on the
 shore of the
 Lollipop Sea
In the garden of
 Shuteye Town.

—Eugene Field

6. Bake a test cookie (see step #7); if the test cookie doesn't crisp up, you may need to add a little more flour to the batter.
7. Drop the batter by spoonfuls onto a non-stick or lightly greased pastry sheet. Bake in the preheated oven for about 16 to 18 minutes or until the cookies are slightly brown on top. Leave plain or brush with the glaze while the cookies are hot.

Makes about 3 dozen cookies

VARIATION:
A few slivered prunes may be added, as both prunes and apricots are compatible with orange juice and either of the liqueurs suggested.

## COOKIE GLAZE

This is nice on any cookie or cake that needs a shiny glaze but not an actual frosting.

1½ cups confectioners' sugar
1 tablespoon unsalted butter, at room temperature
⅛ teaspoon salt
¼ teaspoon pure vanilla extract
About 2½ tablespoons milk, cream, apple juice, apple cider, or Calvados

1.  Using an electric mixer, cream the confectioners' sugar, butter, salt, and vanilla together until the mixture is soft and smooth. Add enough milk or other liquid to make a good spreading consistency.
2.  Using a brush, spread the glaze over the cookies while they are still hot so they will shine.

Makes 1 cup

 Calvados (French apple brandy) is especially delicious in this glaze.

## GINGER AND MARMALADE PUDDING

This is a very old Southern pudding but it's not very well known, which makes it a welcome treat—and it is exceptionally easy to make. You can even cook it ahead and then reheat it just before serving.

*1 cup beef kidney suet, ground*
*4 cups soft fresh bread crumbs*
*2 cups bitter orange or other citrus marmalade*
*2 tablespoons slivered crystallized or preserved ginger*
*2 large eggs*
*1½ teaspoons baking soda*
*¼ cup water, at room temperature*
*2 or 3 cooked prunes, chopped (optional)*
*Anglaise Sauce (recipe follows), for garnish*

1.  Combine the suet, bread crumbs, marmalade, ginger, and eggs in a large mixing bowl. Stir the baking soda into the water until it dissolves and add it to the mixture. Blend thoroughly with an electric mixer. Stir in the prunes by hand if you are using them.

2. Spoon the pudding into a double boiler and cook, covered, over simmering water for 2 hours.
3. Serve the pudding warm in small dessert or custard cups with a garnish of Anglaise Sauce.

Serves 6 to 8

 It is best to use the suet from around the kidneys, as it is less fibrous.

## ANGLAISE SAUCE

This is the true Christmas custard, inherited from our English ancestors. It's historically known as boiled custard and is lovely with pound cake, fruitcake, or your favorite cookie.

*4 cups whole milk*
*3 large eggs, separated*
*3 large egg yolks*
*½ cup sugar*
*⅓ teaspoon salt*
*1½ teaspoons pure vanilla extract or cognac vanilla (see page 29)*
*1 cup whipped cream, for serving*

1. Heat the milk carefully in a saucepan until it is steaming. *Do not allow it to boil.* Remove the pan from the heat.
2. Using an electric mixer, food processor, or whisk, beat the 6 egg yolks with the sugar and salt until the mixture is light and creamy.
3. Add the warm milk and mix thoroughly. Transfer the mixture to a double boiler and cook over simmering water until the custard is thick enough to coat a wooden spoon.

4.   Remove from the heat at once, add the vanilla, and pour the custard into a cool bowl. Place it, covered, in the refrigerator right away. Stir it gently every once in a while to prevent a skin from forming on top.

5.   When the custard is cold, after having chilled in the refrigerator for 1 to 2 hours, beat the 3 egg whites until they are stiff but not grainy or dry—as grainy egg whites will *not* hold up—and fold them into the custard.

6.   Serve immediately with the whipped cream.

Serves  6 to 8

VARIATION:
For the traditional Southern version, add a tablespoon or so of bourbon, rum, or cognac to the custard along with the vanilla.

### ABOUT MAKING CUSTARD

There are some important things to remember when making custard:

• If it is cooked over too high a heat or for too long, it will curdle. Cook over gentle heat and do not overcook.

• Beating the egg yolks with the sugar helps prevent curdling, but be careful not to overbeat.

• The beaten egg whites, added at the last minute, will make the custard a little thicker, but they may be omitted altogether.

• Chilling custard at once helps prevent curdling. (Custard can curdle after it is removed from the stove, since it continues to cook as long as it's hot.)

• Custard keeps well in the refrigerator for several days, but it must be kept in a clean, tightly closed jar. If not, it will pick up flavors from other food and a skin will form on top. If the custard will be in the refrigerator only for a short while, it can simply be covered with plastic wrap.

## MENU 2

*Oyster and Clam Chowder*
Celery Curls, Carrot Sticks, Pickles
*Easy Bread Sticks*
*Colonial Gingerbread*
Coffee

This has always been one of our favorite menus for a relaxed, fun evening of trimming the tree. It is easy and can be cooked and ready before the crowd rolls in.

A delicious homemade soup is one of the most gracious of all foods, with the exception of homemade bread, and Southern cooks are at their happiest making these two themes of glory. Brillat-Savarin, the eminent French gastronome who wrote the famous book *The Physiology of Taste*, is reputed to have said, "A woman who cannot make a good soup should not be allowed to marry." I don't think we dare go that far, but this I know: we do love a good soup.

A fine soup is made of the freshest ingredients available. Leftovers and yesterday's "mistakes" scraped into the pot make an inferior soup. Good cooking is admittedly time-consuming but ever so rewarding, and a great pleasure to your family and friends.

Have plenty of festive celery curls, carrot sticks, pickles, and bread sticks on hand to serve with the Oyster and Clam Chowder. For the crowning touch, serve coffee and pass the homemade gingerbread.

## OYSTER AND CLAM CHOWDER

This chowder makes a wonderful holiday brunch or supper.

2 cups homemade chicken stock
2 cups whole milk
1 cup heavy or whipping cream
3 shallots, peeled and minced, or 2 slices onion
½ red bell pepper, finely slivered
¼ cup water
3 tablespoons unsalted butter
1 pint fresh oysters, chopped, with their juice
1 can (8 ounces) clams, with their juice, or 1 cup minced fresh clams
    plus ½ cup juice (fresh clams come whole and must be minced; canned
    clams are usually pre-minced)
Salt and freshly ground white pepper to taste

*Cayenne pepper to taste*
*3 tablespoons chopped fresh parsley, for garnish*
*2 tablespoons chopped fresh chives, for garnish (optional)*
*Chowder crackers, for serving*

1. Pour the chicken stock, milk, and cream into the top of a large double boiler or into a roomy kettle set over a pan of hot water. Cook, stirring frequently, over a medium heat until hot and thoroughly combined, but *do not allow the mixture to boil*.
2. Combine the shallots, bell pepper, water, and butter in a shallow saucepan. Simmer until the bell pepper and shallots are tender and the water has evaporated, 4 to 5 minutes. Add to the stock mixture.
3. Add the oysters and clams, with their juices, to the stock mixture and stir well. Season to taste with salt, white pepper, and cayenne.
4. Heat the chowder over boiling water until it is just below the boiling point. *Never allow the chowder to boil*. Discard the onion slices if you used them, and taste and correct the seasoning. Sprinkle with the parsley—and the chives, if desired—and serve with chowder crackers.

Serves 6 to 8

VARIATION:
For a richer soup, add 1 or 2 egg yolks just before the chowder is finished. Egg yolks are a more delicate thickening agent than flour and butter (*beurre manié*).

Shallots are always preferred to onions in seafood, but I'll bet the fishermen used onions. And if you like, you can crumble a few chowder crackers into the soup, the way the fishermen always did.

To reheat the chowder, use a double boiler. Don't put the chowder over direct heat, as it will cause the oysters to overcook.

## EASY BREAD STICKS

These crisp and crunchy bread sticks are a song to make, and they're delicious with pasta dishes, salads, and of course chowder!

1 package dry yeast
¾ cup lukewarm water
2 tablespoons extra-virgin olive oil or
    flavorless vegetable oil
1 to 1¼ teaspoons salt
2 cups sifted all-purpose flour
1 egg white, lightly beaten
Coarse (kosher) salt, poppy seeds, or toasted
    sesame seeds, for topping

1. Combine the yeast with the lukewarm water in a roomy mixing bowl and stir to dissolve the yeast.
2. Add the oil to the yeast mixture and blend it in. Add the salt and flour. Mix thoroughly but do not overmix.
3. Toss the dough onto a lightly floured surface and knead it thoroughly, about 2 minutes, adding only enough extra flour to keep the dough from being sticky.
4. Place the dough in a greased bowl and turn it over to grease all sides. Cover the bowl with plastic wrap and leave it in a warm spot to rise until the dough has doubled in bulk, about 1 hour. When lightly touched, the risen dough will spring back at once.
5. Place the dough again on a lightly floured surface and knead it for a few seconds.
6. Roll out the dough to form a rectangle 6 inches wide. Cut it crosswise into strips ¾ inch wide.

7. Roll each strip in the palms of your hands to create a rope and shape it as you like. Place the ropes on a nonstick or lightly greased pastry sheet, cover with plastic wrap, and leave in a warm place until the dough has doubled in bulk, about 1 hour.
8. Meanwhile, preheat the oven to 350°F.
9. Brush the bread sticks with the beaten egg white and sprinkle them with your choice of coarse salt, poppy seeds, or toasted sesame seeds. Bake until golden brown, 25 to 30 minutes.

Makes 15 to 18 bread sticks

VARIATION:
*Crunchy Cornmeal Bread Sticks:* Add ¼ cup fine white cornmeal and reduce the flour to between 1½ and 1⅔ cups. Use coarse salt as the topping.

## COLONIAL GINGERBREAD

This gingerbread came to Virginia from England at the time George III was struggling to hold on to the colonies (or rather, to their taxes). Judging by the stories of his enormous appetite, he could have eaten this entire cake at one sitting. I have to admit, it is terribly good—in fact, I do believe it is the best I've ever tasted. The sorghum molasses is important; do try to find some. I am not sure they used sorghum in eighteenth-century England, but we certainly did in the South.

*1 cup plus 3 tablespoons sifted all-purpose flour*
*1¼ teaspoons ground cinnamon*
*½ teaspoon ground allspice*
*1 teaspoon ground ginger*
*¼ teaspoon ground cloves*
*¼ teaspoon freshly grated nutmeg*

1½ teaspoons baking powder
⅓ teaspoon baking soda
⅓ teaspoon salt
⅓ cup (5½ tablespoons) unsalted butter, at room temperature
⅓ cup light brown sugar
1 large egg, lightly beaten
½ cup molasses (sorghum if possible)
½ cup boiling water
Whipped cream, for topping

1.  Preheat the oven to 350°F.
2.  Lightly grease a 9- or 10-inch springform pan, or a 10 × 8 × 1½-inch cake pan, and line it with foil or wax paper. Set it aside.
3.  Combine the flour, cinnamon, allspice, ginger, cloves, nutmeg, baking powder, baking soda, and salt in a mixing bowl. Mix thoroughly and set aside.
4.  Using an electric mixer, cream the butter and brown sugar in a large bowl until smooth. Beat in the egg and then add the molasses and boiling water. Add the flour mixture and combine thoroughly.
5.  Pour the batter into the prepared pan. Bake for about 35 minutes, until the cake bounces back when lightly touched with your finger or when a knife inserted into the center comes out clean. Allow the cake to cool for about 5 minutes before removing it from the pan (the ginger radiates so much heat that it will make the gingerbread crack open if you unmold it too soon).
6.  Release the sides of the springform pan (or invert the cake pan over a wire rack) and allow the cake to cool slightly.
7.  Serve the cake warm, topped with whipped cream.

Serves 6

You can make the gingerbread ahead, allow it to cool thoroughly, and then freeze it. To serve, thaw the gingerbread and then heat it for 25 to 30 minutes in a 300°F oven.

## ABOUT ALLSPICE

Among the world's many spices, warm, sweet, versatile allspice is the only one that is native to the Western Hemisphere. The tall, beautiful allspice trees were not in bloom when Columbus arrived on his first voyage in search of spices and gold, so he missed them as well.

When it is dried, the allspice berry looks very much like a smooth pepper-corn, and it is considered to taste of three other spices—cloves, cinnamon, and nutmeg—thus its name, "allspice." It is a most welcome spice in our kitchens because of its many talents. It is flavorful with certain meats, soups, and sauces, and it is indispensable in holiday cakes, cookies, and puddings.

## Menu 3

*Beef and Noodle Soup*
*Warm Broccoli, Black Olive, and Roquefort Salad*
French Bread
*A Very Special Chocolate Pudding*
*with Hard Sauce or Foamy Sauce*
Coffee

When Christmas gets too hectic, make a big pot of soup. I have never known a person who doesn't love a good soup— and I never want to meet one, that's for sure!

In the early days, soup was a meal in itself. It was full of good meat and vegetables, simmering away in a big kettle full of flavor and nourishment, quietly awaiting the family to gather around the table and sing its praises.

There was always homemade bread, a relish or two, and preserves— and a bit of dessert with cold milk or hot coffee as a fitting finale to one of our greatest blessings: good food.

Delicious food brings out the best in us. It nourishes our bodies and lends a feeling of well-being as nothing else can.

## Beef and Noodle Soup

This is a basic family soup—flavorful, nourishing, and congenial to variations. If you are fond of wild rice, use it instead of pasta. Then add some wild mushrooms, dried or fresh. A touch of marjoram in the final heating is delicious—mushrooms love marjoram.

3½ to 4 pounds short ribs, brisket, rump, or oxtails,
    cut into ¼-pound pieces
5 quarts cold water
2 medium onions, peeled and left whole
5 ribs celery
2 or 3 carrots
3 imported bay leaves
1 teaspoon dried thyme
½ teaspoon dried sweet marjoram
8 to 10 fresh parsley stems, tied in a bunch with string
6 to 8 peppercorns
1¼ cups peeled and chopped onions
¼ pound homemade fresh noodles or dried pasta, such as
    spaghetti or linguini (broken into smaller pieces) or fusilli
½ large green bell pepper, chopped
½ large red bell pepper, chopped
1 cup chopped fresh parsley
Salt and freshly ground black pepper to taste

1.  Place the short ribs and water in a large soup pot and bring to a low boil. Add the 2 whole onions, celery, carrots, bay leaves, thyme, sweet marjoram, parsley stems, and peppercorns. Simmer for 3 to 4 hours, adding more water if necessary to maintain the same level. Don't use a cover, but watch the soup carefully. Regularly skim off the scum that rises to the surface. Let the stock cool and then refrigerate it, covered, overnight.

2. The next day, skim the congealed fat off the surface of the stock and dis-card the fat along with the vegetables. Remove the meat from the bones, discarding all fat, and chop the meat into small pieces. Set it aside.

3. Strain the stock through a fine-mesh sieve into a large saucepan. Add the chopped onions and bring to a boil. Simmer until the onions are almost tender, about 10 minutes. Then add the noodles and bell peppers and sim-mer until the noodles are tender, 5 minutes for fresh, 10 or so for dried (taste a noodle to check if it's done). Add the reserved chopped beef and chopped parsley and season with salt and pepper. Bring the soup back to a boil.

4. Serve the soup, piping hot, in large soup plates.

Serves 6

VARIATION:
*Beef, Mushroom, and Noodle Soup:* Remove the stems from ¼ to ½ pound fresh mushrooms and add the stems to the stock along with the onions, carrots, and celery in step #1. Omit the bell peppers in step #3. Slice the mushroom caps, sauté them in butter, and add them to the soup when you add the noodles.

Now Christmas comes
 Tis fit that we
Should feast and sing,
 and merry be,
Keepe open house, let
 fiddlers play—
A fig for cold, sing
 care away:
And may they who
 thereat repine
On brown bread and
 on smalle beere dine.

　　—From an old almanac

# Warm Broccoli, Black Olive, and Roquefort Salad

This gorgeous Italian salad combines the salad and the vegetable in one dish. It's delicious with veal roast or chops, broiled chicken, or steak. To turn it into an entrée salad, just before serving sprinkle it with chopped, hot broiled bacon, hot slivers of fried country ham, or thin slivers of chicken breast or steak that have been quickly sautéed in butter.

1 bunch broccoli
2 ounces Roquefort, Maytag blue, or a Danish
　　blue cheese, at room temperature
½ cup mayonnaise
½ cup sour cream
Salt to taste
½ cup black olives, preferably Niçoise
4 hard-cooked eggs
Chopped fresh parsley, chervil, or tarragon
Dijon Vinaigrette Dressing (recipe follows)

1. Peel the stems of the broccoli and divide the bunch into serving-size pieces. Set them aside.
2. Mash the blue cheese and blend it with the mayonnaise and sour cream. Add salt if needed. Set the mixture aside.
3. Bring a pot of salted water to a boil and add the broccoli. Cook until it is crisp-tender, 5 to 6 minutes. It should still be bright green. Drain it well and transfer it to a warm platter, arranging the pieces in a pleasing design.

4. Place the olives in a mound in the center of the platter. Cut the eggs into quarters and arrange them around the platter. Sprinkle the eggs with salt and chopped parsley.
5. Spoon Dijon Vinaigrette Dressing over the warm broccoli and serve the Roquefort mixture separately.

Serves 4 to 6

VARIATION:
If you like anchovies, chop 3 or 4 fillets and add them to the vinaigrette—or pass them separately in a small bowl.

## DIJON VINAIGRETTE DRESSING

The most popular variation of the basic vinaigrette.

*1 egg yolk*
*2 tablespoons white wine vinegar*
*1 tablespoon Dijon mustard*
*¾ cup extra-virgin olive oil*
*Salt and freshly ground white pepper to taste*
*Minced fresh herbs to taste*
*Fresh lemon juice, if needed*

Combine the egg yolk, vinegar, mustard, oil, salt, and white pepper in a jar or blender. Mix well. Stir in the herbs. Taste and add salt and lemon juice if needed.

Makes about 1 cup

The use of sugar in a vinaigrette (or in mayonnaise) is an abomination!

## A Very Special Chocolate Pudding
## with Hard Sauce or Foamy Sauce

This pudding makes a welcome and charming dessert served along with the traditional Christmas puddings and cakes. It is essential to use the best imported chocolate you can find. The guests are asked to make a choice between the sauces, but they never do—they always have some of each.

½ navel orange
6 tablespoons sugar
6 tablespoons (¾ stick) unsalted butter
4 or 5 ounces imported semisweet chocolate
2 large eggs
⅔ cup milk
2 cups sifted all-purpose flour
2½ teaspoons baking powder
⅓ teaspoon salt
1½ teaspoons cognac vanilla (see page 29) or pure vanilla extract
3 tablespoons Cointreau, Jamaica rum, or cognac
Hard Sauce or Foamy Sauce (recipes follow), for serving

1. Butter a 2-quart melon mold and set it aside. Grate the orange zest by hand or remove it with a peeler; combine the zest with the sugar in a food processor and twirl until the zest is finely grated.
2. Combine the butter and chocolate in the top of a double boiler and heat over simmering water until melted.
3. Combine the orange zest and sugar with the eggs in a large mixing bowl and beat thoroughly. Alternating, gradually add the milk and flour, beating thoroughly after each addition. Stir in the melted butter and chocolate. Then add the baking powder, salt, vanilla, and liqueur. Mix thoroughly again.

4. Spoon the mixture into the prepared mold. Place the mold on a rack in a steamer (or in a deep flameproof baking or roasting pan) and add boiling water so that it reaches ⅔ of the way up the sides of the mold. Cook, covered, in simmering water for 1½ hours or until a knife inserted in the center comes out clean.

5. Remove the mold from the steamer and let the pudding cool in the mold for 15 to 20 minutes. Then unmold it onto a serving platter. Serve warm with Hard Sauce or Foamy Sauce.

Serves 6 to 8

## HARD SAUCE

This classic sauce is delicious with a variety of warm puddings. Vary the liqueur to correspond to the flavoring in the pudding—but please, never use a synthetic liqueur.

*½ cup (1 stick) unsalted butter, at room*
   *temperature*
*1½ cups sifted confectioners' sugar*
*6 to 8 tablespoons Cointreau, Jamaica*
   *rum, or cognac*

Combine the butter and confectioners' sugar in a mixing bowl and cream together until smooth. Add the liqueur and blend it in thoroughly. Cover and refrigerate until ready to serve.

Makes about 2 cups

## FOAMY SAUCE

Try this sometime with Grand Marnier. The liqueur adds a marvelous orange-flavored accent.

½ cup (1 stick) unsalted butter, at room temperature
1 cup extra-fine sugar
3 large eggs, separated
¼ teaspoon ground mace
½ teaspoon ground coriander
¼ cup Cointreau, Jamaica rum, or cognac

1.  Combine the butter and sugar in a mixing bowl and beat until creamy.
2.  Add the egg yolks, mace, and coriander and mix thoroughly.
3.  Spoon the mixture into the top of a double boiler and cook it over simmering water, stirring, until thickened.
4.  Remove the pan from the heat and stir in the liqueur.
5.  Beat the egg whites until stiff and fold them into the sauce. Serve cold or at room temperature.

Makes about 2½ cups

### HOW TO MAKE COGNAC VANILLA

This is the supreme vanilla extract—a keystone in baking exceptionally good cakes and cookies. Ounce by ounce, it is not quite as expensive as the so-called pure vanilla available at the market.

To make cognac vanilla, cut a vanilla bean in half lengthwise, exposing the tiny seeds, and then cut the halves into small lengths. Place the pieces (with the seeds) in a bottle containing 4 to 5 ounces of cognac (or brandy) and close it tightly. Shake the bottle every once in a while to free the seeds from the pods. This mixture will keep, at room temperature, for 2 to 3 years, although you can use it immediately. (I do a great deal of baking, so I use 6 vanilla beans in a fifth of cognac.)

The extract will always smell predominantly of cognac, but the vanilla flavor comes gloriously and deliciously alive when it comes in contact with heat. Some cooks use vodka instead of cognac or brandy, but that makes a very poor extract.

# CHRISTMAS EVE SUPPER PARTIES

## MENU 4

Champagne, Chilled White Wine, or Red Wine
Raw Vegetables with *Spicy Dipping Salt*
*Smithfield Ham and Potato Pie*
*Spiced Cranberries*
*Pomegranate and Bibb Lettuce Salad*
*Chilled Bourbon Custard*
*The Yule Log*
Demitasse

The tree is decorated, the stockings are hung, the presents are wrapped—so let's settle down to a quiet family supper that includes one of our favorite savory pies.

## SPICY DIPPING SALT

A dipping salt for raw carrot sticks, celery curls, zucchini strips, and cauliflower or cucumber pieces.

2 tablespoons cumin seeds
2 tablespoons coriander seeds
3 tablespoons sea salt or coarse (kosher) salt
½ teaspoon cayenne pepper

Heat the cumin and coriander seeds in a heavy skillet or in a 350°F oven, just until they have heated through. Transfer the seeds to a blender or spice grinder, add the salt, and grind until fine. Stir in the cayenne pepper.

Makes about ⅓ cup

## SMITHFIELD HAM AND POTATO PIE

All the elements of this pie can be prepared and set aside overnight, then assembled the next day, baked, and served piping hot. With a green salad and dessert, what an elegant Christmas party, and so easy!

4 or 5 large Idaho potatoes
Standard or Flaky Butter Pastry dough for a 2-crust pie (see page 48 or 50)
1 cup slivered baked Smithfield ham, Kentucky country ham, or prosciutto
⅓ cup chopped fresh parsley
3 tablespoons chopped fresh marjoram, or 1½ tablespoons dried marjoram
Salt and freshly ground white pepper to taste
6 tablespoons (¾ stick) unsalted butter
½ cup plus ⅓ cup heavy or whipping cream
1 egg yolk

1. Bring a large pot of salted water to a boil. Meanwhile, peel the potatoes and slice them paper-thin; you should have 4 cups. Drop the potatoes into the boiling water and cook for 3 minutes. Drain at once, cover, and refrigerate.
2. While the potatoes are cooling, preheat the oven to 425°F. Roll half the pastry out ⅛ inch thick and line a 10-inch ovenproof glass pie plate with it, allowing a 1-inch overhang around the rim.
3. Arrange a layer of cooled potatoes in the bottom of the pastry-lined pie plate and sprinkle it with some of the ham, parsley, marjoram, salt, and white pepper. Dot with some of the butter. Repeat the layers until all the potatoes, seasonings, and butter are used up. Pour the ½ cup cream carefully over the potatoes.
4. Roll the top crust out very thin and place it over the pie. Cut a small hole in the center of the crust. Brush the edge of the bottom crust with water and crimp the top and bottom edges together with the tines of a fork. With a sharp knife, trim the crust even with the rim of the pie plate. Brush the top with a little of the remaining ⅓ cup cream.
5. Place the pie plate on the lowest rack in the preheated oven and bake for 50 minutes. If the edges brown too quickly, cover them with strips of aluminum foil; if the top browns too fast, lower the heat to 375°F and cover the pie loosely with foil. When the pie is golden brown on the bottom, remove it from the oven.
6. Mix the egg yolk with the remaining cream. Using a small funnel, pour the mixture very slowly and carefully through the center hole in the crust (you may not need all of the mixture). Return the pie to the oven for another 5 minutes.
7. Allow the pie to cool only for about 5 minutes before serving (it should be served quite hot).

Serves 6 to 8

If you have extra pastry trimmings, cut them into fancy shapes and place them on top of the crust before baking; then brush with cream and bake as directed.

## SPICED CRANBERRIES

This makes a great gift as well as a welcome addition to your Christmas Eve table. It goes well with roast turkey or chicken, and nothing could be easier!

*4 cups cranberries*
*1 tablespoon grated lemon zest*
*2½ cups sugar*
*½ cup water*
*1 cinnamon stick, about 3½ inches long*
*2 tablespoons fresh lemon juice*
*½ teaspoon ground cloves*

1. Pick over the cranberries, discarding any soft ones. Set them aside.
2. Combine the lemon zest with the sugar in a food processor and twirl until the zest is finely grated (or grate the zest by hand and add it to the sugar).
3. In a large saucepan, combine the zest and sugar with the water, cinnamon stick, lemon juice, and cloves. Bring to a boil and cook for 5 minutes. Add the cranberries and boil for 12 to 15 minutes, until a thick sauce has formed. Set aside to cool.
4. When cool, refrigerate until ready to serve. (It will keep for a week in the refrigerator, or you can freeze it.)

Makes 3½ to 4 cups

## POMEGRANATE AND BIBB LETTUCE SALAD

The pomegranate, or Chinese apple, is the perfect fruit for our very special Christmas salads. It comes on the market just as the winter chill sets in and we begin to think about our holiday menus. It is a fruit of the Eastern world—China, Persia, Greece. It has never been a well-known fruit in the United States except in the days gone by when grenadine was made of real pomegranates. We still have grenadine, but now it is a blend of ingredients.

The red pulp and shiny, glistening seeds of the pomegranate are delicious, but tedious to prepare. This salad, however, is so beautiful and utterly delicious and festive that it is worth the trouble for special occasions. The pomegranate, as you no doubt have noticed, was a favorite fruit in Old Master paintings.

*2 pomegranates*
*¼ cup white wine vinegar*
*3 teaspoons dry mustard*
*Salt to taste*
*¾ cup vegetable oil or extra-virgin olive oil*
*1 or 2 small shallots, peeled and minced*
*Pinch of sugar (optional)*
*3 heads Bibb lettuce*
*Watercress or parsley sprigs, for garnish*

1.  Cut the pomegranates in half and scoop out the seeds and pulp (be careful not to get any of the bitter white pith). Put the seeds and pulp in a small bowl, cover, and set aside.
2.  In another small bowl, mix together the vinegar, mustard, and salt. Slowly add the oil, blending thoroughly. Stir in the shallots.

3. Add the vinaigrette to the reserved pomegranate and mix well. Taste for salt. Add a tiny pinch of sugar if it is needed. Cover and refrigerate overnight or for as long as 24 hours if you're preparing it ahead of time.
4. Cut the Bibb lettuce heads in half and, keeping the halves intact, rinse them gently and pat dry. Arrange the lettuce halves on salad plates so that the shadings of yellow and green are well displayed. Spoon a few tablespoons of the pomegranate dressing over the lettuce and garnish with sprigs of watercress.

Serves 6

Never wash Bibb lettuce until just before you are going to serve it; the lettuce is very tender and bruises easily. And never soak it in water—just give it a gentle rinse.

## CHILLED BOURBON CUSTARD

This old-fashioned dessert can be made several days ahead—just cover it and keep it in the refrigerator until serving time.

6 large egg yolks
¼ cup sugar
1 teaspoon all-purpose flour
Pinch of salt
2 cups milk
1 or 2 tablespoons good-quality bourbon
Whipped cream, sweetened to taste, for garnish
Freshly grated nutmeg, for garnish (optional)

1. Place a medium-size ceramic or stainless-steel bowl in the refrigerator to chill.
2. In a heavy saucepan that is not made of aluminum, combine the egg yolks, sugar, flour, and salt. Beat until the mixture is pale yellow.

3.  Warm the milk in a small saucepan. Place the egg yolk mixture over a medium heat and slowly stir in the warm milk. Cook, stirring constantly with a whisk or wooden spoon, until the custard coats a wooden spoon rather heavily, 4 to 5 minutes.
4.  Immediately pour the custard into the chilled mixing bowl (this stops the cooking), cover, and place in the refrigerator until it is cold, about 2 hours. Do not stir the custard while it is chilling. When the custard is thoroughly chilled, stir in the bourbon.
5.  Serve in custard cups, topped with sweetened whipped cream. Sprinkle a little nutmeg over the whipped cream if you like.

Serves 4 to 6

Beating the egg yolks thoroughly with the sugar and other dry ingredients before adding the warm milk helps prevent curdling.

## THE YULE LOG

The story of the Yule log goes back to the time of the Saxons and the Goths, who commemorated the festival of the winter solstice by burning a huge log. The log was lit with a piece of wood carefully saved from the last year's log. This ceremony was meant to bring good fortune to the entire family during the coming year.

This is probably the most delicious of all chocolate cakes. It is a tradition in northern Italy, where it is called *Ceppo di Natale* and served just after midnight mass on Christmas Eve.

### WHIPPED CREAM FILLING
*1½ cups heavy or whipping cream*
*2 tablespoons cognac or Grand Marnier*
*Sugar to taste*

## CAKE
5 tablespoons water or coffee
7 ounces semisweet chocolate or dark sweet chocolate
6 large eggs, separated
1 cup sugar
1½ teaspoons pure vanilla extract or cognac vanilla (see page 29)
½ cup cocoa
White edible flowers, such as violas, pansies, or tea roses, for garnish

1. Preheat the oven to 350°F.
2. Whip the cream until it holds a soft peak. Fold in the cognac and add sugar to taste. Cover and place in the refrigerator until ready to use.
3. Add the water or coffee to the chocolate in the top of a double boiler. Cook over simmering water until the chocolate has melted, stirring until smooth. Remove from the heat and let cool a bit.
4. Beat the egg yolks and sugar with an electric mixer until they are a light shade of yellow and look like mayonnaise. Add the chocolate to the egg yolks and sugar. Mix well and add the vanilla.
5. Beat the egg whites until they are stiff but not dry or grainy. Carefully fold them into the chocolate mixture using a rubber spatula.
6. Grease a 15½ × 10½-inch pastry sheet with vegetable shortening and then line the pastry sheet with foil, leaving a few inches overhanging at each end. Grease the foil.
7. Spread the batter evenly over the prepared pastry sheet. Place the pastry sheet on the middle rack of the preheated oven and bake for 15 to 17 minutes or until the cake springs back when touched. Open the oven door and allow the cake to stand in the oven for 5 minutes longer.
8. Remove the cake from the oven and cover it with a clean, damp cloth (this keeps the top from forming a crust). Place the cake in the refrigerator or allow it to cool on the counter until it reaches room temperature.
9. When cool, carefully remove the cloth and loosen the cake from the sides of the pastry sheet. Dust the top generously with the cocoa.

10. Turn out the cake, cocoa-covered top down, on a piece of heavy-duty foil. Carefully peel off the foil on which the cake was baked.
11. Spread the whipped cream filling evenly over the cake.
12. Lift the foil on one of the longer sides, which will cause the cake to lift as well, and roll the cake away from you, as you would a jelly roll. Roll the log onto a long, narrow silver or white platter. Cover with foil and refrigerate until ready to serve.
13. Just before serving, garnish the cake with edible flowers.

Serves 6 to 8

VARIATION:
After spreading the whipped cream filling over the cake, spoon 3 tablespoons good-quality raspberry preserves down the middle of the filling. It's awfully good and not very expensive.

## MENU 5

*Mulled Red Wine*
Champagne, Chilled White Wine, or Red Wine
*Country Ham Baked in Cider*
*Spiced Pear and Cranberry Relish*
*Baked Brown Rice with Almonds or Pine Nuts*
*Kentucky Bourbon Pie*
*Best-Ever Pumpkin Pie*
*Frozen Lemon Soufflé*
Demitasse

F ew Christmas menus could be more Southern or more festive than this one, which is a favorite of my family. We adore country ham and all the dishes that go with it—and of course I hope you will find them very special, too.

## MULLED RED WINE

This is a festive and delicious punch that complements beef, ham, or game.

*Zest and juice of 2 lemons*
*Zest and juice of ½ navel orange*
*2 cups cold water*
*7 or 8 whole cloves*
*1 cinnamon stick (3 inches long)*
*¼ cup sugar*
*1 bottle good-quality red wine*

1. Warm 12 to 15 punch cups.
2. Finely sliver the lemon and orange zest. Strain the lemon and orange juices into a stainless-steel saucepan. Add the zest, water, cloves, cinnamon stick, and sugar.
3. Pour in the wine and heat the mixture until it is very hot, but *do not allow it to boil*. Strain the wine into a heated pitcher and then pour it into the warm punch cups and serve immediately.

Serves 12 to 15

## COUNTRY HAM BAKED IN CIDER

There are few things in life more enjoyable to the palate of a true Southerner than a country ham, and a small amount of apple cider is the only flavor I know that provides a good counterpoint to country hams. In any case, the cider is to be used as an occasional spice. It is also quite a flavorful addition to commercial hams, which of late have had little to savor.

1 smoked country ham (12 to 15 pounds)
1 gallon apple cider
2 teaspoons ground cloves
½ cup light brown sugar
1 teaspoon dry mustard
Watercress sprigs, for garnish

1. Have the butcher cut off the ham hock if desired. Scrub the ham thoroughly with a stiff brush.
2. Place the ham in a large, deep pan such as a roasting pan and cover it completely with cold water. Let it soak for at least 12 hours or as long as 24.
3. When the ham has finished soaking, preheat the oven to 325°F.
4. Remove the ham from the roasting pan and discard the water in which the ham has been soaking. Place the ham, fat side up, back in the roasting pan. Cover it completely with a mixture that is equal amounts apple cider and water. Place the pan on the lowest rack in the preheated oven and cook for 2 hours. Do not allow the liquid to exceed a quiet simmer; if it starts to boil, reduce the heat to 300°F (too high a heat will toughen cured meat).
5. Turn over the ham and cook another 2 hours (20 to 25 minutes per pound total cooking time) or until an instant-reading thermometer registers 170°F.
6. Remove the ham from the oven but leave it in the cider-water overnight (this helps keep the ham moist).
7. The next day, preheat the oven to 425°F. Discard the cider-water and remove the skin from the ham. Sprinkle the ground cloves over the fat. Blend the brown sugar with the mustard, adding enough apple cider to make a thick paste. Brush the paste over the top of the ham and bake for 20 to 25 minutes, until the ham has a beautiful golden glaze. Allow it to cool.
8. To serve, slice the ham very, very thin and arrange it on a large platter. Garnish with watercress.

Serves 15 to 20

VARIATION:
If you like, you can surround the ham with poached apples as well as sprigs of watercress.

## SPICED PEAR AND CRANBERRY RELISH

Pears are among our most delicious and versatile winter fruits. This relish will add zest and sparkle to many holiday menus— turkey, chicken, ham, game, or savory pies.

*2 cups cranberries*
*1 cup water*
*1 cup sugar*
*1 small piece fresh or dried ginger root*
*1 or 2 firm Kiefer, Anjou, or Bosc pears (barely beginning to ripen)*
*Juice of 1 lemon, or to taste*

1. Pick over the cranberries, discarding any soft ones. Set them aside.
2. Combine the water, sugar, and ginger root in a large saucepan and bring to a boil. Reduce to a simmer and cook for about 5 minutes.
3. Peel and core the pears, cut them into eighths, and add them to the saucepan. Cook for 3 to 5 minutes, until the pears are barely tender.
4. Add the cranberries and cook until they have popped and cooked into a sauce, 10 to 15 minutes. Remove from the heat. Discard the ginger root and stir in the lemon juice. Allow the relish to cool.
5. Cover and refrigerate. The relish will keep for several days.

Makes about 2 pints

## BAKED BROWN RICE WITH ALMONDS OR PINE NUTS

The unique flavor of pine nuts or the crunchy texture and nutty flavor of almonds are most pertinent to brown rice. Either variation is delicious with pork, chicken, game, or veal dishes.

*3 tablespoons plus ¾ tablespoon unsalted butter*
*1 cup uncooked brown rice*
*1½ cups homemade chicken stock*
*1 imported bay leaf*
*1 or 2 sprigs fresh thyme, or ½ teaspoon*
*dried thyme*
*Salt and freshly ground white pepper to*
*taste*
*⅓ cup almonds or pine nuts (the almonds*
*should be slivered, but the pine nuts can*
*be used whole)*

1. Preheat the oven to 350°F.
2. Melt 1½ tablespoons of the butter in a heavy ovenproof saucepan. Add the rice and stir until the grains are coated with butter. Add the stock, bay leaf, and thyme sprigs. Season to taste with salt and white pepper.
3. Cover the saucepan with a tight-fitting lid and place it on the middle rack of the preheated oven. Cook until the rice is tender but not mushy (taste it to be sure), 1 to 1½ hours.
4. Put the nuts in a heavy skillet with the ¾ tablespoon butter over a medium heat. Toss until a light brown. Set aside.

5. Remove the pan from the oven and discard the bay leaf and thyme sprigs. Using a fork to fluff the rice, stir in the remaining 1½ tablespoons butter and the toasted nuts. Mix well and serve immediately.

Serves 4

VARIATION:
Toasted, chopped cashews or macadamia nuts can be substituted if desired.

Lundberg is a good brand of brown rice. Organically grown, it is large grained, nutty, and delicious. You can find it at health food stores and gourmet shops. Pine nuts should be toasted before using, as they are raw when purchased.

## KENTUCKY BOURBON PIE

Very fine aged bourbon tastes a great deal like brandy, and some of our finest bourbons have vanilla in their formula. I bring out this flavor by adding my own homemade cognac vanilla to this pie.

Kentucky Bourbon Pie should not be made until the day it is to be served; otherwise the crust will soften.

4 teaspoons gelatin
2 tablespoons cold water
¾ cup sugar
7 large egg yolks
3 tablespoons boiling water
Grated zest of 1 lemon
3 tablespoons fresh lemon juice
½ cup best-quality Kentucky bourbon
1½ cups heavy or whipping cream

*4 large egg whites*
*1 teaspoon pure vanilla extract or cognac vanilla (see page 29)*
*1 Standard Pastry 10-inch pie shell (see page 48), baked*
*Preserved kumquats or fresh kiwi fruit, for garnish*

1. In a small bowl, stir the gelatin into the cold water. Set it aside to soften.
2. In a heavy saucepan, combine ½ cup of the sugar with the egg yolks and beat until the mixture is smooth and pale yellow. Place the pan over a medium heat and heat thoroughly; *do not allow the mixture to boil*. Remove the pan from the heat.
3. Stir the boiling water into the softened gelatin and mix thoroughly. Add the gelatin to the egg mixture, along with the lemon zest and juice. Add the bourbon and mix well.
4. In a chilled bowl, whip the cream until it is stiff. Set aside one quarter of the whipped cream and fold the rest into the egg mixture.
5. In a separate bowl, beat the egg whites until they form stiff peaks. Gradually add the remaining ¼ cup sugar, beating until the whites form a stiff meringue. Fold them gently into the egg mixture. Stir in the vanilla.
6. Spoon the filling evenly into the baked pie shell and refrigerate until firm, 2 to 3 hours.
7. To serve, cut the pie into wedges and garnish with preserved kumquats or a few slices of kiwi. Serve the remaining whipped cream separately (or you can use it to garnish the pie before slicing it).

Serves 8

## BEST-EVER PUMPKIN PIE

One of the glories of the fall and winter seasons in the Deep South, especially during the Christmas holiday, is pumpkin pie. When the snow covers the ground and the cold air chills our bones, what could taste better or make us feel happier than to share with friends and loved ones our favorite pies? Dress up the pie with a touch of whipped cream, if you like, but don't ever forget the coffee.

2 cups best-quality canned puréed pumpkin
1 cup heavy or whipping cream
3 large eggs
1 cup sugar
1 teaspoon salt
1¼ teaspoons ground cinnamon
¾ teaspoon ground ginger
¼ teaspoon ground allspice
¼ teaspoon ground cloves
¼ teaspoon freshly grated nutmeg
1 teaspoon pure vanilla extract or cognac vanilla (see page 29)
1 Standard or Flaky Butter Pastry 10-inch pie shell (recipes follow),
    partially baked and cooled
2 tablespoons unsalted butter
Whipped cream, for topping

1.  Preheat the oven to 400°F.
2.  Measure the pumpkin into a roomy bowl. Add the cream and eggs and beat thoroughly with a whisk.
3.  In a small bowl, combine the sugar, salt, and spices. Toss them together well. Beat into the pumpkin mixture. Add the vanilla and mix thoroughly.
4.  Spoon the filling into the partially baked and cooled pie shell. Dot with the butter.
5.  Place the pie on the lowest rack of the preheated oven and bake for 8 to 10 minutes, then lower the heat to 350°F and continue to bake the pie until a knife inserted in the middle comes out clean and the crust is light golden brown, about 45 minutes.
6.  Allow the pie to cool slightly before serving. Pass the whipped cream separately.

Serves 8

VARIATION:

*Sweet Potato Pie:* Substitute mashed, cooked sweet potatoes for the pumpkin. Unlike pumpkin pie, sweet potato pie usually has a meringue on top. The choice is yours.

Good-quality canned puréed pumpkin is easier to use than fresh pumpkin. Like melons, pumpkins are a gamble — they can be very stringy.

An ovenproof glass pie plate is by far the superior pan for pies, as one can see clearly when the bottom crust has browned sufficiently.

A partially baked crust makes for a crisper final crust than when a raw crust is used.

## STANDARD PASTRY

This is the classic American pie crust. It is made with vegetable shortening, which is a hard fat, so it is not as easy to blend or roll as butter pastry — but it is more economical and not as rich. There are certain times when this is the perfect pastry for that very reason: for instance, pecan pie and several other Southern pies that are on the sweet side need the blandness of the vegetable shortening crust. (Lard, which has been used in the South for pastry for several hundred years, does make a lovely crisp crust, but vegetable shortening is excellent and more in favor today.)

*2 cups sifted all-purpose flour*
*1 teaspoon salt*
*⅔ cup solid vegetable shortening, chilled*
*6 to 8 tablespoons ice water*

1. Sift the flour and salt together into a mixing bowl. Using a pastry blender, cut the shortening into the flour until the mixture resembles coarse meal.
2. Sprinkle 6 tablespoons of the ice water over the flour a little at a time, blending it in quickly and lightly with your fingers; then squeeze the dough together. Work fast, as the mixture must stay cold. If the dough is not soft enough to form into a ball easily, add a little more water.
3. Form the dough into a ball and cut it in half. Roll out one half on a lightly floured surface or pastry cloth. (If you are not going to use it at once, cover the dough with foil and refrigerate until you're ready to use it—but it's easier if you roll it out at once.)
4. As soon as the dough is rolled out, fit it into the pie plate. Cover it with foil and refrigerate or freeze until you are ready to use it.
5. Roll out the other half of the dough for the top crust. Place it on a baking sheet lined with wax paper, cover it with foil, and refrigerate or freeze it.

Makes 2 crusts

## PROPORTIONS FOR A 1-CRUST PIE

*1½ cups sifted all-purpose flour*
*¾ teaspoon salt*
*½ cup solid vegetable shortening, chilled*
*3 to 6 tablespoons ice water*

If the pastry feels hard and is difficult to roll, you didn't use enough water. If it is as soft as biscuit dough and becomes tough when baked, you used too much.

## FLAKY BUTTER PASTRY

This is the quintessential butter pastry. It does not rank second to puff paste—it stands alone. With a versatility few crusts have, it is still the easiest of all to blend and roll, and the flavor is unsurpassed. This is the pastry I teach first to a new student, and it always remains a favorite. Use it especially for apple, rhubarb, peach, or strawberry pie.

Golden as a winter sunset,
Light as a fleecy cloud,
Luscious as a sun-kissed
   berry
That, my friend, is pie.

—Unknown

2¼ cups sifted all-purpose flour
¾ teaspoon salt
14 tablespoons (1¾ sticks) unsalted butter, chilled
      and cut into small pieces
⅓ cup ice water, or as needed

1. Sift the flour and salt together into a mixing bowl. Using a pastry blender, cut the pieces of butter into the flour until the mixture resembles coarse meal.
2. Sprinkle the ice water over the flour mixture a little at a time, blending it in quickly and lightly with your fingers; then squeeze the dough together. Work fast, as the mixture must stay cold. If the dough is not soft enough to form into a ball easily, add a little more water.
3. Form the dough into a ball and cut it in half. Roll out one half on a lightly floured surface or pastry cloth. (If you are not going to use it at once, cover the dough with foil and refrigerate until you're ready to use it.)
4. As soon as the dough is rolled out, fit it into the pie plate. Cover it with foil and refrigerate or freeze until you are ready to use it.
5. Roll out the other half of the dough for the top crust and place it on a baking sheet lined with wax paper, cover it with foil, and refrigerate or freeze it.

Makes 2 crusts (see following page for 1-crust proportions)

## PROPORTIONS FOR A 1-CRUST PIE

This recipe will give you a little extra dough, but don't try to change the proportions. Use the extra to make turnovers.

*1 cup plus 2 tablespoons sifted all-purpose flour*
*Pinch of salt*
*7 tablespoons unsalted butter, chilled and cut into small pieces*
*½ cup ice water, or as needed*

If the pastry feels hard and is difficult to roll, you didn't use enough water. If it is as soft as biscuit dough and becomes tough when baked, you used too much.

### HOW TO ROLL OUT PASTRY

1. Make up the dough for a 2-crust pie and divide it in half. Wrap one half in foil and refrigerate it.
2. Place the other half of the dough on a lightly floured surface. Flatten it a bit with a rolling pin. Then roll out the dough lightly, working from the center to the edges and lifting the rolling pin on each stroke as it nears the edge. Dust the dough with flour to keep the rolling pin from sticking or use a rolling pin stocking that has been dusted very, very lightly with flour. Continue until you have formed a circle large enough to extend 1 inch over the edge of the pie plate. The pastry should be thin—never more than ⅛ inch thick. If possible, the bottom crust should be *very* thin.
3. Roll up the pastry on the rolling pin, lift it over the pie plate, and unroll it. Using your fingers, fit the pastry loosely into the plate (this keeps the dough from shrinking below the edge of the plate). Fill the pastry as desired.

4. Following step #2 again, roll out the other half of the dough. Roll it up loosely on the rolling pin, place it over the filled pie, and unroll it.

5. Moisten the edge of the bottom crust with water and then press the top and bottom edges together. Trim off the excess dough with a sharp knife, pressing the edges together firmly. Use the tines of a fork to press the edges down around the rim of the plate (or flute the edges).

6. Make a few slits in the top crust with a sharp knife to allow steam to escape and bake as directed.

To flute the edges, place your right index finger on the inside rim of the pastry, and your left index finger and thumb on the outside of the pastry. Press your fingers together. Repeat, working your way around the rim of the pie plate, to form a wavy (fluted) edge. This edge has a greater tendency to over-brown than an edge that's pressed flat.

Remember: pastry dough must be kept cold or it won't be flaky when baked.

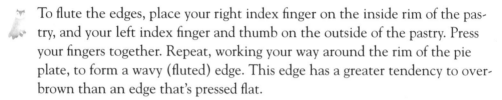

## FROZEN LEMON SOUFFLÉ

Few flavors are as refreshing as lemon, and in this frozen soufflé we have the perfect light but zestful dessert.

6 large eggs, separated
1 cup sugar
7½ tablespoons fresh lemon juice
Grated zest of ½ lemon
Dash of salt
1½ cups heavy or whipping cream
8 thin lemon slices, seeds removed, or small fresh mint leaves, for garnish (optional)
¼ cup unsalted pistachio nuts, chopped, for garnish (optional)

1. Combine the egg yolks with the sugar in a large mixing bowl and beat with a whisk or an electric mixer until they turn a lighter shade of yellow and fall in ribbons from a spoon. Add the lemon juice and zest.
2. In another large bowl, beat the egg whites with the salt until they hold a stiff peak. Fold them into the yolk mixture.
3. In another bowl, beat the cream until it holds a soft peak. Fold it into the egg mixture, mixing thoroughly.
4. Make a foil collar for a 5- or 6-cup soufflé dish; the collar should be about 4 inches wide. Brush the top 3 inches of the collar with vegetable oil. Using string, tie the collar around the soufflé dish so that it stands 2 inches above the rim.
5. Spoon the mixture into the prepared soufflé dish and freeze it for 8 hours or as long as overnight.
6. Remove the foil collar. About an hour before serving, garnish the top of the soufflé with curled lemon slices or small fresh mint leaves and, if you like, a sprinkling of chopped pistachios.

Serves 8 to 10

Now Christmas is come,
Let us beat up the drum
And call all our neighbors
 together;
And when they appear,
Let us make them
 such cheer
As will keep out the wind
 and the weather.

—Washington Irving

## MENU 6

Champagne or Chilled White Wine
*Brie and Red Bell Pepper Pie*
Italian Bread
*Bibb, Endive, Artichoke, and Prosciutto Salad*
*Bartlett Pear and Pineapple Sherbet*
*White Christmas Truffles*
Demitasse

This is a Christmas Eve supper that I believe even the Roman general and epicure Lucullus would have loved—salad served with Italian bread and featuring a good cheese, wine, and a bite of yummy dessert.

## BRIE AND RED BELL PEPPER PIE

W hen this savory pie comes from the oven, all puffed up in its glory and beauty, it is the gourmet's dream come true.

*Flaky Butter Pastry dough for a 9-inch 1-crust pie (see page 50)*
*9 ounces Brie or Camembert cheese*
*½ cup finely slivered red bell pepper*
*2 tablespoons unsalted butter*
*2 large eggs*
*1 large egg yolk*
*⅔ cup heavy or whipping cream*
*Salt to taste*
*Cayenne pepper to taste*

1. Preheat the oven to 400°F.
2. Line an ovenproof glass pie plate with the pastry, allowing a little slack for the pastry to shrink slightly, and trim the edges.
3. Remove the rind from the cheese and chop the cheese. Sprinkle the cheese and bell pepper over the pastry. Dot with the butter.
4. Combine the eggs, egg yolk, and cream thoroughly with a whisk. Season with salt and cayenne and spoon over the cheese.
5. Place the pie on the lowest rack of the preheated oven and bake for about 35 minutes or until the top and the crust are golden brown. The pie is done when a knife inserted a few inches from the center comes out clean.
6. Serve the pie warm.

Serves 6 to 8

The cheese must be absolutely fresh for this pie.

Flaky Butter Pastry is best for this pie, and it can be made ahead, left unbaked, wrapped in foil, and frozen.

## BIBB, ENDIVE, ARTICHOKE, AND PROSCIUTTO SALAD

Tarragon is considered the king of culinary herbs and it has a great affinity for artichokes and asparagus, to say nothing of prosciutto and the divine Belgian endive and our famous Kentucky Bibb lettuce.

The cheese-mites asked how
the cheese got there,
And warmly debated the
matter;
The orthodox said it came
from the air,
And the heretics said from
the platter.

—Old English verse

3 heads Bibb lettuce
2 heads Belgian endive
3 artichoke bottoms, cooked
⅓ to ½ pound prosciutto or baked country ham,
thinly sliced
⅓ to ½ pound asparagus spears, cooked
3 tablespoons fresh tarragon leaves
2 tablespoons chopped fresh parsley
3 tablespoons white wine vinegar
1 or 2 teaspoons Dijon mustard
Salt and freshly ground white pepper to taste
½ cup extra-virgin olive oil

1. Rinse and dry the Bibb lettuce and the endive.
2. Slice the artichoke bottoms and sliver the prosciutto. Cut each asparagus spear into 3 pieces. Line a large salad bowl with the greens and arrange the artichokes, prosciutto, and asparagus on top. Sprinkle the tarragon and parsley over the salad.

3.   In a small bowl, stir together the vinegar, mustard, salt, and white pepper. Slowly add the olive oil, stirring constantly. Pour this dressing over the salad, toss gently, and serve.

Serves 4 to 6

### ABOUT PREPARING ARTICHOKE BOTTOMS

Break off the artichoke stems. (This permits any fibrous strings to be pulled out. If the stems are sliced off, the strings remain in the bottom of the artichoke.) Tear off all the tough outer leaves, pulling each one back and down toward the base.

Using a small, sharp stainless-steel (not carbon steel) knife, neatly pare the bottom where the stem has been torn off. Don't worry about the chokes at this point.

The pared surface of an artichoke darkens rapidly when in contact with the air, so it is best to rub it with the cut surface of half a lemon several times during the preparation process.

Fill a stainless-steel or enamel saucepan with water, bring it to a boil, and add the juice of half a lemon, a pinch of dried thyme, and a pinch of salt. Plunge the pared artichokes into the boiling water and cook at a simmer until the flesh no longer resists a sharp knife or the tines of a cooking fork, 10 to 30 minutes depending on the quality and age of the artichokes. Don't overcook them; they should remain firm.

Remove the pot from the heat and let the artichokes cool in the liquid (well submerged), covered and refrigerated, until ready to use.

Using a teaspoon or small ice tongs, gently pry loose the chokes. Pat the artichoke bottoms dry with a kitchen towel and proceed with your recipe.

## BARTLETT PEAR AND PINEAPPLE SHERBET

This elegant sherbet, like all sherbets and ice cream, is much creamier when made in a mechanical freezer, but it does come out rather well when you follow these directions.

*1½ cups sugar*
*1 cup water*
*4 ripe Bartlett pears, or 1 can (8 ounces)*
   *pears, drained*
*Juice of 3 or 4 lemons (up to ½ cup), to taste*
*2 cups crushed fresh pineapple, or 1 can*
   *(20 ounces) unsweetened crushed pineapple*
*3 tablespoons French pear brandy or Cointreau*
*Fresh mint sprigs or kiwi fruit, for garnish*

1.  Combine the sugar and water in a small saucepan and bring to a boil. Boil until the syrup is clear, about 2 minutes. Then refrigerate until cold, at least 2 hours, or chill in the freezer for 1 hour.
2.  Peel the pears and discard the cores. Combine the pears and lemon juice in a food processor or blender and purée (this helps to retard darkening). In a stainless-steel bowl, combine the pear purée, cooled sugar syrup, and crushed pineapple. Mix thoroughly and taste for sugar and lemon. Freeze the sherbet for 6 to 8 hours or as long as overnight.
3.  When the sherbet is frozen, beat it with an electric hand mixer until the mixture whitens and is fluffy. Return it to the freezer until you are ready to serve it.
4.  Serve in sherbet glasses or glass bowls, garnished with a spoonful of brandy and a sprig of mint or several slices of kiwi fruit.

Serves 6 to 8

## ICE CREAM AND SHERBET

Ice cream, sherbet, and nearly all frozen mixtures of fresh fruits, fruit juices, and cream are without a doubt mankind's favorite and oldest desserts.

Frozen fruit desserts were created by the Chinese centuries ago. They in turn gave the recipes to the Persians, the Arabians, and the East Indians. It was hundreds of years, however, before these desserts became known in the West. Culinary historians contend that they were first introduced in France around 1660 by an Italian named Procopia. And Marco Polo, the most famous of the early adventurers, is supposed to have brought the idea back to Italy from his travels in the East.

Measured by today's standards, those early frozen dishes couldn't have been really delicious, but the idea was ingenious. Before the nineteenth century, all ice creams and sherbets, from the Chinese down to the French and Italians, were frozen by placing the ingredients in a container that was then placed in another, larger container filled with ice, and mixed either by shaking the liquid, by stirring it with a large spoon, or by turning the smaller container by hand. These desserts were, of course, soft and grainy; they did not have the firm texture of today's frozen desserts, but they nevertheless held an esteemed place on the menu and were made only in the wealthier homes.

Although ice creams and sherbets are not truly American, we adore them and have figured largely in their refinement. It was, for instance, an American housewife named Nancy Johnson, a New Englander, who in 1846 invented the first hand-turned wooden ice-cream freezer. Mrs. Johnson surrounded the container that held the ice-cream mixture with crushed ice and salt and cranked away, and the modern ice-cream freezer with paddles was born.

# White Christmas Truffles

I f you are one who enjoys a small glass of brandy after a lovely dinner, do make these truffles! With a good cup of coffee—I should say a demitasse—they make a memorable occasion linger a long while.

## TRUFFLES
1 tablespoon candied orange peel, finely chopped
1½ tablespoons Cointreau, Grand Marnier, or Mirabelle
1 pound white chocolate, finely chopped
1 cup heavy or whipping cream

## COATING
1 pound white chocolate, finely chopped

1. Make the truffles: combine the candied orange peel and ½ tablespoon Cointreau in a small bowl and set aside to marinate for at least 1 hour or as long as overnight.
2. Place the white chocolate in the top of a double boiler and set over simmering water. Stir with a wooden spoon until the chocolate has melted and is smooth, 10 to 15 minutes.
3. Bring the cream to a full boil in another saucepan, stirring it often. Pour the hot cream over the melted chocolate and stir until the mixture is smooth. Remove it from the heat.
4. When the chocolate mixture has cooled a bit, add the remaining 1 tablespoon Cointreau and the marinated peel with its liqueur. Let cool to room temperature.
5. Line a baking sheet with aluminum foil or wax paper. Shape the chocolate mixture into small balls. Arrange them on the baking sheet and refrigerate until thoroughly chilled, about 1 hour.

6. Coat the truffles: melt the white chocolate in the top of a double boiler. Remove it from the heat and allow it to cool slightly. Using a fork, dip each truffle into the melted chocolate so it is well covered. Lift the truffle and let the excess chocolate drip back into the double boiler (you can gently tap the fork on the side of the pan to remove more chocolate—this helps prevent a "platform" of chocolate from forming under the finished truffle). Place the coated truffles on a foil-lined baking sheet. Refrigerate until they are thoroughly chilled, at least 1 hour.
7. Arrange the truffles in fluted foil or paper cups made for the purpose (available at candy supply stores) and store them in a single layer in an airtight container. (They freeze well.)

Makes about 40 truffles

VARIATION:
Substitute 1 tablespoon French kirsch or pear liqueur for the marinated orange peel. (The pear liqueur is called *poire eau-de-vie*, and *eau-de-vie* means "water of life.")

# CHRISTMAS MORNING BREAKFAST

## MENU 7

Fruit Juice

Broiled Bacon or Sausage

*Old-Fashioned Buttermilk Waffles with Tangerine Syrup*

*German Apple Pancakes*

*Wonderful Cranberry Preserves*

Black Bing Cherry Preserves

*Very Special French Toast with Cinnamon
and Coriander Mélange*

Coffee, Tea

One of life's most sustaining and delightful pleasures is when the family gathers at the breakfast table, not only for the good food but also for the camaraderie and inspiration of being together. Because of the fast pace of life nowadays, this graciousness has almost faded away.

But let us save what we can. Christmas breakfast comes to my mind as a perfect hour to be with one another, to gather in the warmth of the kitchen as of old, to taste again the wonderful pancakes and waffles adorned with your own homemade syrup. Oh, yes, they do contain a cache of luscious calories, but such fun doesn't come along every day.

## OLD-FASHIONED BUTTERMILK WAFFLES WITH TANGERINE SYRUP

These waffles can be made a few days ahead and frozen in anticipation of Christmas morning breakfast. Just cook them, let them cool, and then stack four or five together with wax paper between them. Wrap the stacks in foil and freeze. When the big morning arrives and a few other things are going on, all you have to do is pop the waffles in the toaster!

*2 cups sifted all-purpose flour*
*2¼ teaspoons baking powder*
*½ teaspoon baking soda*
*½ teaspoon salt*
*1 tablespoon sugar*
*3 large eggs, separated*
*2 cups buttermilk*
*½ cup (1 stick) unsalted butter, melted*
*Tangerine Syrup (recipe follows), for serving*

1. Stir together the flour, baking powder, baking soda, salt, and sugar in a large mixing bowl.
2. In another bowl, combine the egg yolks, buttermilk, and melted butter. Mix well and add to the flour mixture. Beat hard with a whisk (you can use an electric mixer, but be careful not to overbeat, which will dry out the batter).

3.   Beat the egg whites until they hold a stiff peak but are not grainy. Gently fold them into the batter and mix well.
4.   Cook the waffles in your waffle iron and serve hot. Pass the Tangerine Syrup.

Serves 4

VARIATION:
*Sour Cream Waffles:* Use 1 cup sour cream and 1 cup buttermilk. These waffles will be a bit "shorter," crisper.

Naturally, the waffles are at their best when first made, but freezing them ahead of time works better than one might think, and on Christmas Day cooks need all the help they can muster!

## TANGERINE SYRUP

This wonderful and simple recipe can easily be doubled.

*10 to 12 large tangerines*
*½ cup sugar, or to taste*
*1½ teaspoons cornstarch*
*1 teaspoon fresh lemon juice, or to taste*
*1 tablespoon unsalted butter*

1. Squeeze the juice from the tangerines and strain it into a medium-size non-reactive saucepan.
2. In a small bowl, stir together the sugar and cornstarch. Add the mixture to the tangerine juice and bring it to a boil. Cook until the syrup has thickened and become transparent, about 5 minutes.
3. Stir in the lemon juice and butter. Remove the pan from the heat and serve hot.

Makes about 2 cups

> If you make the syrup ahead of time, store it in the refrigerator in a heavy 1-pint canning jar. Then when you're ready to serve it, place the jar in a pan of water and heat it until the butter has melted and the syrup is good and hot. (The syrup will keep indefinitely.)

## GERMAN APPLE PANCAKES

It is much easier and faster to make these apple pancakes in the oven for a holiday crowd than to make regular pancakes on a griddle. Best of all, these baked pancakes are very delicious and a special treat for a holiday breakfast—or any winter breakfast, to be truthful. You'll see!

4 tablespoons (½ stick) unsalted butter, for the skillets
Zest and juice of 1½ lemons
2 or 3 large apples (Gala, Golden Delicious, or Winesap)
4 large eggs
1 cup sifted all-purpose flour
1 teaspoon salt
2 tablespoons sugar
1 cup milk
4 tablespoons (½ stick) unsalted butter, melted
¾ cup sifted confectioners' sugar, for dusting
Lemon and orange wedges, for serving (optional)

1.  Preheat the oven to 400°F. Coat two 9- or 10-inch ovenproof skillets with the 4 tablespoons butter.
2.  Grate the lemon zest and squeeze the juice.
3.  Core, peel, and cut the apples into uniformly thin slices. Place the slices in a large mixing bowl and add the lemon zest and juice. Mix carefully.
4.  In a large bowl, beat the eggs with an electric mixer until fluffy. Gradually add the flour, salt, and sugar, alternating with the milk. Beat until the mixture is smooth.
5.  Divide the batter between the 2 prepared skillets. Cover the batter with the apples and sprinkle with 2 tablespoons of the melted butter.
6.  Place the skillets on the middle rack of the preheated oven and bake for 15 to 20 minutes. Then reduce the heat to 350°F and bake until the pancakes are well done, puffed around the sides, and a pleasing golden brown. Watch carefully so they do not get too brown. (If your oven's too small to get both skillets on one shelf, bake the pancakes one at a time.) Remove from the oven and sprinkle with the remaining 2 tablespoons melted butter.
7.  Transfer the pancakes to warm platters and sprinkle with the confectioners' sugar. Cut each pancake into 6 or 8 wedges and serve. If you like, pass lemon and orange wedges for everyone to squeeze over their serving.

Serves 6 to 8

VARIATION:
Add 2 tablespoons ground cinnamon to the confectioners' sugar.

 I use Corning flameproof glass skillets for these pancakes because it's so easy to check on the browning through the glass. Old-fashioned black iron skillets work fine too, though.

If your breakfast crowd is smaller, cut the recipe in half. That'll serve 4 people—unless they are growing boys!

## WONDERFUL CRANBERRY PRESERVES

For the Christmas breakfast table, or serve with whole-wheat pancakes, waffles, or English muffins. A great gift idea: tie a waffle or pancake recipe to a jar of the preserves with a merry red-and-green ribbon. Black Bing Cherry Preserves are also a wonderful gift—see page 227 for the recipe.

*4 cups cranberries*
*2 navel oranges*
*3 cups sugar*
*2 teaspoons fresh lemon juice*
*2 cups water*
*Pinch of salt*
*½ cup coarsely chopped walnuts (optional)*

1. Pick over the cranberries, discarding any soft ones. Set them aside.
2. Peel the zest from the oranges and combine the sugar and zest in a food processor. Twirl until the zest is finely grated (or grate the zest by hand and add it to the sugar).

3.  Cut the oranges in half and discard the seeds. Remove the orange pulp by sections, using a sharp knife, and place it in a large saucepan. Add the zest and sugar along with the lemon juice, water, and salt. Bring to a quiet boil and cook for about 10 minutes.
4.  Add the cranberries and cook rapidly until the mixture reaches the jellying point or until a candy thermometer registers 221°F. Add the walnuts if you're using them and cook until they're heated through, about 1 minute.
5.  Spoon the preserves into hot sterilized jars and seal at once, or spoon them into freezer jars (only ¼ full) and freeze.

Makes about 2 pints

To test preserves or jelly without a candy thermometer, dip a cool metal spoon into the boiling mixture. Raise the spoon at least a few inches above the pan, out of the steam, and turn it so the jelly runs off the side. If the jelly forms two drops that flow together and fall off the spoon in one sheet, it is done.

## VERY SPECIAL FRENCH TOAST WITH CINNAMON AND CORIANDER MÉLANGE

This French toast is a favorite with everyone who tastes it. It must be made from a loaf of brioche or rich challah (egg bread), and it must be made with heavy cream so it will puff. Milk or so-called half-and-half will not do. This is a perfectly delicious holiday breakfast or brunch served with good coffee and a sausage that contains no garlic whatsoever.

The French toast is best, of course, when first made, but I often sauté a few extra slices, wrap them in foil, and refrigerate them. When I'm ready to serve them, I place them in a preheated 400°F oven for about 6 minutes, watching them carefully. They seem to puff up just a little again.

*2 large eggs*
*½ cup heavy or whipping cream*
*6 tablespoons (¾ stick) unsalted butter, more if needed*
*4 slices brioche or challah, each 1 inch thick*
*Cinnamon and Coriander Mélange (recipe follows) or confectioners'*
*    sugar, for sprinkling*

1.  Preheat the oven to 400°F.
2.  Beat the eggs in a large bowl until they are fluffy. Add the cream and mix thoroughly.
3.  Melt 3 tablespoons of the butter in a nonstick skillet. Dip 1 slice of the brioche quickly into the egg mixture and place it in the sizzling butter (if your skillet is large enough, do 2 slices at a time). Cook, shaking the skillet, until the toast is lightly browned, 2 or 3 minutes. Turn and lightly brown the other side, another 2 minutes (do not let the slices get hard and crusty). Repeat with the remaining slices.
4.  When all the slices have been browned, bake them in the preheated oven until they are slightly puffed, about 5 minutes. Serve at once, sprinkled with some Cinnamon and Coriander Mélange or confectioners' sugar.

Serves 4

  Don't let the bread sit in the egg mixture or the toast will be soggy. Just dip the slices quickly and then slip them into the skillet.

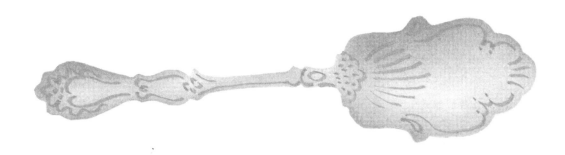

## CINNAMON AND CORIANDER MÉLANGE

This sweet mixture of sugar and spice is delightful on French toast. Try it also on cinnamon toast, sweet muffins, or sugar cookies. It's the coriander that sets it apart from other cinnamon sugars.

*1½ teaspoons ground cinnamon*
*½ teaspoon ground cloves*
*1½ teaspoons ground coriander*
*1½ cups sugar*

Combine all the ingredients and mix thoroughly. The mélange will keep indefinitely if stored in a clean jar at room temperature.

VARIATION:
Substitute light brown sugar for half of the granulated sugar.

### THE CUP THAT CHEERS

All the world loves coffee, the cup that soothes and cheers, and its story is one of romance and intrigue.

If you would start the day with felicity, what could surpass a delicious breakfast and a cup of hot coffee? It tastes so good, and it strengthens us for the hustle of the day's work that lies ahead.

"This little bean is the source of happiness and wit," said Dr. William Harvey, the noted English physician, speaking of coffee in a prophetic mood in 1657. He bequeathed fifty-six pounds of coffee beans (a rare and luxurious gift at the time) to the London College of Physicians, directing that his friends gather once a month to drink coffee in his memory. Coffee was considered a medicine in those days and was carried in the doctor's kit.

Coffee has a long and fascinating history, rather chimerical in its way. The origin of coffee remains shrouded in myths and stories of the Arabs and the Middle East. It seems well established, however, that coffee was native to Ethiopia. At least one thousand years ago, some traders brought coffee beans across the Red Sea into Arabia, where the Muslim monks had already cultivated coffee trees in their gardens.

Another story tells of Kaldi, an Ethiopian goatherd who one day noticed that his goats were frolicking and nibbling gaily at a cluster of shiny dark leaves on a shrub bearing red berries. When Kaldi tasted the berries, he too found them very vivifying. Kaldi shared his discovery with the inhabitants of a nearby monastery. The good brothers developed a fondness for the coffee berries (which they did not roast, but simply boiled in water) and found they could stay awake even during evening prayers.

Another legend attributes the discovery of coffee to Omar, an Arabian dervish who was exiled to the wilderness, where he faced starvation. But Omar survived by making a broth from the coffee berries.

Now you are free to believe what you will, of course, but I love culinary tales shaded by the mysteries of past centuries.

The coffee tree blooms with white flowers that are scented like jasmine. It's not uncommon for the fragrant white blossoms, green berries, and ripe red cherries to appear at the same time on the same branch of a coffee tree. The delicate blossoms last only a few days. Then, six to nine months later, the coffee beans, called cherries, appear. The cherries ripen from green to yellow, then to red.

Although technically an evergreen shrub, the coffee plant is generally referred to as a tree, as it will grow to more than twenty feet in height if not pruned. It is, of course, one of the world's great travelers, as it grows in so many countries; but it is at its best in tropical and subtropical climates and high altitudes. It is probably happiest on the slopes of Mt. Kilimanjaro, near the Kenyan border in Tanzania, at 19,300 feet above sea level. High in the clouds with its branches open to the sun and cold winds, it produces one of the finest coffees in the world, the Arabica, known as Kenya A.A.

Coffee became one of America's favorite hot beverages when our country was still a group of thirteen colonies. Originally the early settlers were tea drinkers, a habit they inherited from the English. But when George III kept imposing such stiff taxes on tea imports, the colonists rebelled. One December night in 1773, a group of men disguised as Indians dumped three hundred chests of tea (Twinings, too, they say) into the Boston harbor. In 1775 the colonists voted to ban tea completely. Coffeehouses sprang up everywhere. They became meeting places for politicians, artists, musicians, and journalists, not unlike (but not as elite as) the coffeehouses in England, France, and Italy. Today there is a renaissance of interest in coffee of all kinds, flavored and unflavored, with great enthusiasm for different brews, like the espresso and cappuccino of Italy.

The open-pot method of brewing coffee — the way Kaldi and Omar and the monks brewed it — is simply to pour boiling water over the beans (unroasted, of course, in earlier times) and allow the infusion to steep a few minutes. The Arabs eventually learned to roast and grind the beans, and then coffee truly came into its own.

Somewhere along the way the granite pot with a spout came into being. It was used in our early country kitchens, over campfires, and on the wagon trail to the West. Later on came the percolator, with the gurgling rhythm of the boiling water flowing back and forth over the ground coffee. The fragrance of the steam pouring out of its curved spout is one of the most appetizing aromas we know. Could it be that this most appealing of perfumes is redolent of the coffee tree's jasmine blossom? Maybe not, but no other coffeemaker can arouse our senses of smell and taste quite the same way.

But time marches on, and now we have the French press, which makes divine coffee and is so charming to use and present — it rivals the ceremonial tea hour. The French press goes back to a crude but useful Belgian invention of 1896, which was improved by an Italian named Calamani in 1930. Then, in 1933, a clever bartender in Milan was inspired to redesign and improve the Calamani pot. After World War II, restaurants, specialty shops, and gastronomes quickly adopted the new coffeemaker. It was in truth an Italian invention, but the French embraced it heartily, and no wonder, as it is so efficient and attractive. So it became known as the French press. When quality roasted beans are used, the French press makes wonderful coffee, especially in the Melior pot.

Good coffee enlivens our thoughts in the morning, and in its own inimitable way it is a quieting finale to a good winter supper. And even more: serve it in lovely demitasse cups on a silver tray in front of a dreamy log fire with friends or loved ones, or just by yourself with a good book and soft music. A cup of good coffee is a marvelous thing.

## A Choice of Grinds

| | |
|---|---|
| **Turkish grind** | A flourlike grind used for brewing in an *ibrik* (a Turkish coffeemaker) |
| **Espresso grind** | A very fine grind used primarily for espresso and cappuccino |
| **Fine grind** | Used for all cone-shaped filters and Neapolitan drip pots |
| **Drip grind** | Slightly coarser than fine grind, used for all electric drip brewers with basket-shaped filters |
| **Medium grind** | Slightly coarser than drip grind; usually used for plunger pots, drip pots, and cold water extraction brewers |
| **Coarse grind** | Used for percolators, urns, and most types of open-pot brewing |

## Hints for Making Good Coffee

• Whether you like a rich or a mild blend, delicious coffee must be made full strength. Unlike tea, coffee cannot be "stretched."
• For each serving, use 2 tablespoons of coffee to 6 fluid ounces of fresh, clear water for a strong, full-bodied brew.

• Coffee is at its peak of flavor immediately after brewing. Serve it at once, piping hot. Never, never boil coffee again after it has been brewed.

• Picking the grind is of great importance, as it must be appropriate for the type of coffeemaker you are using. The grind must be fine enough for the water to circulate freely so as to extract the full flavor of the coffee.

# A Hearty Holiday
# Breakfast or Supper

## Menu 8

*Corned Beef Hash with Creamy Hot Mustard*
*or Lorenzo Sauce*
Poached Eggs
*Cottage Cheese Yeast Biscuits*
*Especially Delicious Pear Preserves*
Fruit in Season
Coffee

In the early days, meat was preserved simply by packing it in dry salt—a process we learned from our British forebears. The salt used for preserving was very coarse, like grains of corn, so the process was called "corning."

Other methods of preservation, including corning meat in brine, have long since replaced the dry-salt cure for meat, but the name "corned beef" has stuck. When corned beef is cooked with potatoes, carrots, and cabbage in a broth, we call it a "New England boiled dinner."

The English call leftover corned beef and cabbage "bubble and squeak"—an utterly charming name for an utterly gloomy dish. Cold corned beef and cabbage does make a little squeak as it reheats in a skillet, but squeak or no squeak, we prefer our leftover corned beef made into hash—crunchy brown hash served with a poached egg, hot buttered biscuits, and lots of coffee!

## CORNED BEEF HASH WITH CREAMY HOT MUSTARD OR LORENZO SAUCE

When a hearty meal is in order, there are few breakfast dishes more welcome than corned beef hash. Allspice and ginger lend this recipe a magic touch and flavor, and once again make us aware of the importance of spices used wisely.

2 cups freshly cooked corned beef, finely chopped
1 small onion, peeled and coarsely chopped
3 potatoes, peeled and coarsely chopped
2 tablespoons chopped fresh parsley
⅛ teaspoon ground ginger
¼ teaspoon ground allspice
Salt and freshly ground black pepper to taste
4 tablespoons solid vegetable shortening
Parsley sprigs, for garnish
Creamy Hot Mustard or Lorenzo Sauce (recipes follow)

1.  Place the corned beef in a large bowl and mash it with a fork (this will help it form a solid cake, making it easier to turn).
2.  Bring a large saucepan of salted water to a boil, add the onion and potatoes, and simmer until they are tender, about 35 minutes. Drain, chop fine, and add to the corned beef. Add the parsley, ginger, allspice, salt, and pepper. Toss thoroughly. Taste and correct the seasonings if necessary.
3.  Melt 1 tablespoon of the shortening in a heavy 4- or 6-inch nonstick skillet over a medium-high heat. When the shortening is hot, add one quarter of the hash, pressing down on it with a wooden spoon or a spatula to make it compact. Cook until the hash is brown on the bottom. Loosen the hash with a spatula, invert a plate over the skillet, and turn the skillet upside down, flipping the hash onto the plate. Keep the plate in a warm oven while you cook the remaining hash.
4.  Garnish the hash cakes with sprigs of parsley and serve with Creamy Hot Mustard or Lorenzo Sauce.

Serves 4

The potatoes should be hot when you add them to the corned beef so they mash a bit; this helps the hash form a thick cake.
You can use canned corned beef in this recipe.

## CREAMY HOT MUSTARD

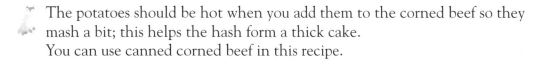 This is somewhat fiery, but very flavorful. Try it also with short ribs, brisket, or hamburgers.

2 tablespoons dry mustard
6 tablespoons cold water
1 cup sour cream
2 teaspoons cider vinegar
Salt to taste

1. Combine the mustard and cold water in a small bowl and beat until the mixture thickens a bit. Set it aside for 20 minutes (this allows the mustard to lose a little of its tang).
2. Add the sour cream, vinegar, and salt. Serve cold or at room temperature.

Makes 1½ cups

 This mustard will keep, covered and refrigerated, for a week.

## LORENZO SAUCE

Lorenzo Sauce is believed to have been created at the Ritz Hotel in Paris by Louis Diat. It is delicious served with a number of meats, especially tenderloin, but I find it pleasing on Corned Beef Hash also.

*½ cup good-quality chili sauce*
*2 tablespoons vinaigrette dressing, made with 4 parts oil to*
     *1 part vinegar*
*⅓ to ½ cup finely chopped watercress*
*Salt to taste*

Mix the chili sauce, vinaigrette, and watercress in a small bowl. Add salt to taste. Serve immediately, at room temperature.

Makes about 1 cup

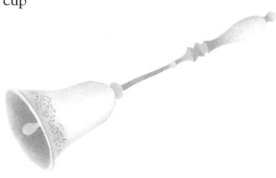

## COTTAGE CHEESE YEAST BISCUITS

You will be delighted with these cottage cheese biscuits. They are not only delicious but very versatile as well, and best of all, they freeze well.

I have a large wooden bowl with sloping sides that I have used for years for making pastry and bread. It is so comfortable to work in because there's plenty of room to mix the dough by hand without spilling. I prefer it to a flat board. Maybe it's not as professional, but it is easier—and anyway, who cares?

1 package dry yeast
½ cup warm water
3½ cups sifted all-purpose flour
2¼ teaspoons baking powder
⅛ teaspoon baking soda
1½ teaspoons salt
1 tablespoon sugar
3 tablespoons unsalted butter, chilled and cut into small pieces
1 cup large-curd cottage cheese
1 large egg
½ cup (1 stick) unsalted butter, melted

1.  Combine the yeast and warm water in a small bowl and stir to dissolve the yeast. Set it aside.
2.  Stir together the flour, baking powder, baking soda, salt, and sugar in a large bowl. Using a pastry blender, cut the 3 tablespoons cold butter into the flour until the mixture resembles fine meal.
3.  Place the cottage cheese in a food processor and process until it is smooth and lump-free. Add the egg and blend thoroughly.
4.  Add the dissolved yeast and the cottage cheese to the flour mixture and stir well. Transfer the dough to a lightly floured surface and knead it thor-

oughly with your hands. Add a little extra flour if the dough is sticky—but don't let it become overly dry or the biscuits will be tough.

5.  Place the dough in a lightly greased bowl and turn it to coat the entire surface. Cover the bowl with aluminum foil or plastic wrap and leave it in a warm place until the dough has doubled in bulk, about 1 hour.

6.  Preheat the oven to 375°F.

7.  Punch down the dough and place it on a lightly floured surface. Knead it again for 2 minutes. Roll it out to a thickness of ⅛ to ¼ inch and cut out the biscuits with a biscuit cutter. Dip each biscuit into the melted butter and place them on a nonstick or lightly buttered pastry sheet. (Don't let the edges touch.) Cover the biscuits lightly with a kitchen towel and set them aside to rise until they spring back at once when lightly touched, 30 to 40 minutes.

8.  When they have risen, transfer the biscuits to the middle rack of the preheated oven and bake until golden brown, 20 to 25 minutes. Serve at once.

Makes about 24 biscuits, depending on the size of the cutter

VARIATIONS:

*Rosemary Biscuits:* Work ½ to 1 teaspoon crushed dried rosemary into the dough after the first rise.

*Watercress Biscuits:* Work ½ to ⅔ cup chopped watercress leaves into the dough just before rolling it out. Bake at once (don't freeze these biscuits).

*Country Ham Biscuits:* Work ½ cup very thinly slivered baked country ham into the dough when you are kneading it after the first rise.

These biscuits freeze well. Roll out the dough, cut out the biscuits, dip them in the melted butter, and arrange them on a pastry sheet and place in the freezer. When the biscuits are thoroughly frozen (this will take several hours), transfer them to plastic bags, seal the bags, and return them to the freezer. When you're ready to use them, place the frozen biscuits on a pastry sheet and let them thaw and then rise until doubled in bulk. Bake as directed.

Rising dough should be left in a warm spot, but not too warm—72°F to 75°F is ideal. If the dough rises too fast, the enzymes in the flour won't have time to develop their flavor.

## BISCUITS

The Marquis François Jean de Chastellux, a French major general traveling in America in 1780, wrote home that the little *galettes* served to him at supper were very much to his taste and that they were evidently easily kneaded and baked on short notice. These pleasing little *galettes* were, of course, our American biscuits.

Despite culinary fashions that come and go, biscuits have remained intrinsically American and are notably well suited to many of our truly American menus. We love them for breakfast with ham or sausage and eggs, and no one has discovered a better companion to country-fried chicken and gravy than the buttermilk biscuit so beloved in the South.

Biscuits made with sweet milk and baking powder are still revered in New England, and rightfully so. Pray tell me, what could taste better with a clam and oyster stew, or lobster chowder, or a Black Angus steak, medium-rare with lots of freshly ground pepper and a crisp cabbage and parsley slaw? Almost nothing.

From the sourdough biscuits that were made on the wagon trail going West to the crackerlike beaten biscuits of tidewater Virginia, down to the golden egg biscuits made so easily in our food processors—all sing of America. From our country kitchens to the White House, biscuits speak of home. Marquis de Chastellux, it has been more than two hundred years, but the little *galettes* still have a lovely taste.

## ESPECIALLY DELICIOUS PEAR PRESERVES

Few relishes or preserves are better with a menu of country ham, good-quality fried ham, sausage, turkey, quail, chicken, or guinea hen than these preserves for the Christmas holiday table. The spiced variation is my favorite.

*6 firm ripe pears (about 2 pounds), such as Kiefer, Bosc,*
    *or Seckel (see owl, next page)*
*3 cups cold water*
*3 cups sugar*
*1 lemon, seeded and thinly sliced*

1.  Peel and core the pears and cut them into eighths.
2.  Combine the water and 1½ cups of the sugar in a large saucepan. Bring to a rapid boil and cook for 2 minutes. Add the pears, reduce the heat, and simmer, uncovered, for 15 minutes.
3.  Add the remaining 1½ cups sugar and the lemon slices to the pears. Stir thoroughly to help dissolve the sugar. Cover and let stand overnight, or for as long as 24 hours, for the pears to soften and plump (either in the refrigerator or at room temperature).
4.  Return the pan to the heat and bring to a boil. Remove the pears with a slatted spoon and pack them into hot sterilized jars. Cook the syrup until it reaches 222°F on a candy thermometer, 5 to 10 minutes, and then pour it over the pears, leaving a ¼-inch headspace. Process in a hot water bath for 10 minutes and seal, or cool and refrigerate or freeze. Leave the preserves for 3 to 5 weeks before using them.

Makes about 5½ pints

VARIATIONS:

*Spiced Pear Preserves:* When you add the sugar in step #3, add three 1-inch pieces of cinnamon stick, ½ teaspoon ground cloves, ½ teaspoon ground coriander, and 1½ teaspoons dried ginger or chopped crystallized ginger.

*Apple Preserves:* Hard, tart apples can be preserved using this recipe.

Bartlett pears are too soft to use in this recipe. If you use little Seckel pears, peel them but leave them whole, with their stems intact, and add a small piece of preserved or crystallized ginger to each jar before sealing.

## PRESERVES

Making fruit jellies, preserves, and marmalades is to me the most charming way of extending the magic of summer.

Preserves, of course, taste their very best when they are first made. There is an essence and fragrance of flavor at that moment that is irreplaceable. I remember so vividly when I was young, spreading a well-buttered slice of bread with spoonfuls of Mother's jelly or jam that hadn't quite settled down yet or cooled from the heat—and how good it was, a fleeting moment of exquisite joy.

It is a wonderful thing, however, that now those flavors, even though a bit diluted, can be frozen in time, as it were, to be kept for special occasions or gifts or just for yourself with tea on a gloomy afternoon.

# CHRISTMAS DAY DINNERS

## MENU 9

Champagne
Caviar on Toast Points
*Roast Suckling Pig*
*Roast Turkey Breast Lined with Country Ham*
*Spiced Moro Oranges*
*Spiced Walnuts on Watercress*
*Shredded Brussels Sprouts*
*Four-Star Cornmeal Butterflake Biscuits*
*Kentucky Eggnog Ice Cream*
*Mother's Ambrosia*
*Plum Pudding Pie*
*Chocolate Almond Toffee*
Demitasse

It was in the fourth century that Pope Julius I of Rome decreed December 25 as the date that was to be set aside each year to celebrate the birth of Jesus Christ.

In France, the main Christmas meal is served on Christmas Eve, immediately after midnight mass; they call it the *réveillon*. But in Britain, it is Christmas Day that is celebrated more in culinary splendor, and we in America have followed suit. The very best of everything that we can muster is our goal for Christmas Day.

## ROAST SUCKLING PIG

Roast suckling pig is one of the glories of an elaborate Christmas celebration. Not only is it delectable, but its flavor blends smoothly on our palates when served with the other dishes of a traditional holiday meal.

I do not like a "carnival"-decorated roast pig, but a small piglet stuffed very simply with apples and a few cloves, then roasted to a glistening golden brown and presented on a bed of crisp watercress with a small red apple in its mouth. This makes Christmas dinner an impressive adventure for both the cook and the diners—and a conversation piece without peer.

The memory of a certain suckling pig will stay with me always. One Christmas years ago, the Junior League, to raise money for charity, had a cooking contest for men only. One young "chef" had roasted a small pig to perfection. It was the dish that won my heart, but not the blue ribbon! The young chef came to me after the votes were counted, almost with tears in his eyes. "But Camille," he said, "I fed that little pig two tablespoons of Spanish sherry twice a day for a week so he would be simply delicious." Now, that brought tears to *my* eyes!

1 piglet, 3 to 5 weeks old (the younger the better), prepared for cooking
1 lemon, cut in half, or 3 tablespoons Spanish sherry or Madeira
Salt and freshly ground black pepper to taste
2 or 3 apples, peeled and cored but left whole (tart apples hold up better)
A few whole cloves
1 teaspoon dried rosemary, or 1 sprig dried sage leaves
2 tablespoons unsalted butter, melted, or 2 tablespoons extra-virgin olive oil
1 small red apple, for garnish
Several bunches fresh watercress, for garnish
Spiced Moro Oranges (see page 90), for garnish

1. Preheat the oven to 450°F.
2. Rinse the piglet thoroughly inside and out in 3 changes of water. Dry it thoroughly inside and out. Rub the inside well with the lemon halves or sherry. Season the piglet inside and out with salt and pepper. Place the peeled apples, cloves, and rosemary in the cavity.
3. Close the cavity by inserting skewers on each side of the opening and lacing them together with strong thread to form a tight seal. Pull the front legs together and tie them securely. Pull the rear legs backward and tie them securely. Put a small wedge of clean wood in the mouth to hold it open. Brush the entire piglet with the melted butter.
4. Place the piglet on a rack in a large roasting pan and cook in the preheated oven until it begins to brown, about 30 minutes. Then reduce the heat to 350°F and continue to roast, basting, for 3½ to 4 hours. The piglet is done when an instant-reading meat thermometer inserted in the thickest part of the leg or loin registers 155°F to 160°F (don't let the thermometer touch the bone). Remove the piglet from the oven.
5. Remove the piece of wood from the mouth and replace it with the small red apple. Line a large carving board with a generous bed of watercress and set the piglet on it.

6.   To carve the piglet, first remove the small hams and slice them. Then cut down the backbone and remove the head (send it to the kitchen!). Carve the rib and loin sections into chops. Arrange some watercress and cooked apple around each serving and garnish with the oranges.

A 10-pound piglet serves 8 to 12

VARIATION:
If you like, serve A Very Special Mustard Sauce (recipe follows) and poached apples with the suckling pig.

   If the piglet is browning too fast, cover it loosely with foil and reduce the oven temperature a bit. (If you prefer, the piglet can be roasted the entire time at 350°F for about 30 minutes per pound.)

# A VERY SPECIAL MUSTARD SAUCE

This mustard sauce is one of the best homemade sauces I know. It can be used in many ways, especially on sandwiches and delicate cold meats such as broiled or grilled chicken and pheasant breasts.

*¼ cup turbinado or granulated sugar*
*3 tablespoons dry mustard*
*4 tablespoons white wine vinegar or rice vinegar*
*2 large egg yolks*
*8 tablespoons (1 stick) unsalted butter, in 1-tablespoon pieces*
*Salt to taste*

1.   Combine the sugar and mustard in the top of a double boiler. Let it rest to allow the bitterness of the mustard to quiet down. Don't start cooking it until the pungency dissipates.
2.   Add the vinegar and mix it in thoroughly.

A man might then behold
A Christmas in each hall
Good fires to curb the cold
And meat for great and
  small
The neighbors were finally
  bidden
And all had welcome true;
The poor from the gates
  were not chidden
When this old cap
  was new.

— Christmas carol

3. Add the egg yolks, 1 at a time, beating hard with a whisk, and place over simmering water. Add the butter, a little at a time, beating hard until the mixture thickens and coats a wooden spoon rather heavily.
4. Add salt to taste and pour into a sterilized 1-pint jar. Cover and refrigerate until ready to use. (Because of the yolks, this sauce should be kept for only a few days.)
5. To heat the sauce, place the jar in a pan of simmering water. Serve warm.

Makes 1 pint

## ROAST TURKEY BREAST LINED WITH COUNTRY HAM

Like many other birds, the turkey has a tendency to dry out if it's not cooked carefully. A heavy coating of butter will keep the meat moist and enhance its flavor. Don't sell butter short—it's one of the finest flavoring agents we have.

**DRESSING**
1 cup white bread cubes, lightly toasted in a 300°F oven
⅓ cup unsalted butter, melted
½ cup chopped celery hearts
1 teaspoon dried marjoram
1 teaspoon dried thyme
1 to 1½ cups roasted whole chestnuts (see owl, below)

## TURKEY

½ lemon or 4 tablespoons Spanish sherry
1 whole fresh turkey breast (6 to 7 pounds)
Salt and freshly ground white pepper to taste
4 or 5 paper-thin slices baked Kentucky country ham,
    Smithfield ham, or prosciutto
⅓ cup unsalted butter, melted
1½ cups homemade chicken stock, or as needed

1.  Preheat the oven to 350°F.
2.  Combine the dressing ingredients in a mixing bowl and toss them lightly with a fork.
3.  Squeeze the lemon half over the cavity of the turkey breast and season it with salt and white pepper.
4.  Line the cavity of the breast with the slices of ham. Fill the cavity with the dressing. Brush the outside of the breast with the ⅓ cup melted butter and season it with salt and white pepper.
5.  Place the turkey breast on a rack in a large roasting pan and cook for 25 to 30 minutes per pound (2½ to 3½ hours) or until a meat thermometer inserted into the thickest part registers 160°F to 165°F. While the turkey is cooking, baste it often with the stock to keep it moist and browning evenly. Brush the pan drippings over the breast and use extra butter if needed.

Serves 10 to 12

The smaller turkey breasts are the most flavorful and succulent ones.

You can find jars of roasted whole chestnuts, imported from France, in gourmet and specialty food stores. They're expensive but worth it.

## SPICED MORO ORANGES

The Spanish Moro orange, also known as the blood orange, which is shipped to our U.S. markets in midwinter, has received a great deal of gourmet interest because of its deep red color, which is new to us and makes it very attractive. The flavor of the blood orange is slightly less acidic than that of the regular orange, but it can be spiced and served as a charming and delicious garnish for suckling pig, duck, goose, roast pork, turkey, or hot ham, or used on turkey sandwiches for festive leftovers.

6 to 8 Moro (blood) oranges
1 cup dry red wine
½ cup water
3½ cups sugar
1½ teaspoons whole cloves
1 teaspoon ground coriander
2 or 3 cinnamon sticks (3 to 4 inches long), broken into thirds

1. Wash the oranges thoroughly and cut them into ¾-inch-thick slices. Put the slices in a saucepan, cover with water, and bring to a low boil. Simmer until tender, about 45 minutes. Drain.
2. Combine the wine, ½ cup water, sugar, and spices in a large saucepan and boil for 5 minutes. Add the drained orange slices and boil gently until they are clear and well glazed, 12 to 15 minutes.
3. Using a slatted spoon, transfer the orange slices to hot sterilized jars. Pour the boiling-hot syrup over the oranges and seal the jars (or allow to cool and refrigerate or freeze).

Makes enough to garnish a large turkey or ham

If you wish, navel or Temple oranges or tangelos may be used, but the Moro orange makes a beautiful red garnish for meats and fowl on special occasions such as Christmas.

## SPICED WALNUTS ON WATERCRESS

If you used up all your watercress with the suckling pig, serve these spiced walnuts over mesclun (baby lettuces) or a mixture of small lettuces such as Bibb, radicchio, arugula, chicory, and endive. And if there are any leftovers, the mixture makes a fabulous sandwich for a light lunch or even for cocktail time!

*1 cup shelled whole walnuts, preferably English walnuts*
*1 tablespoon unsalted butter*
*1½ tablespoons sugar*
*1 teaspoon curry powder*
*Cayenne pepper to taste*
*3 tablespoons Worcestershire sauce*
*Enough watercress for a large bed*

1. Chop some of the walnuts coarsely, leaving about 2 tablespoons in large pieces.
2. Melt the butter in a noncorroding skillet and add the walnuts. Cook them until very lightly toasted, 1 or 2 minutes, tossing them frequently to coat with the butter. Be careful not to let them burn the least bit.
3. Add the sugar, curry powder, and cayenne and mix thoroughly. Then add the Worcestershire sauce and stir over a very low heat until the walnuts have a very thin dark glaze.
4. Let the nuts cool to room temperature and then serve them on a bed of crisp watercress.

Serves 10 to 12

## SHREDDED BRUSSELS SPROUTS

**B**russels sprouts have been the most maligned of vegetables, and all because they have been overcooked. If Brussels sprouts are cooked quickly, they retain their pleasing yellow-green color and crisp texture. With long cooking, they develop an unpleasant strong flavor and lose their fresh color.

½ cup (1 stick) unsalted butter
Cayenne pepper to taste
2 pints firm green Brussels sprouts
1 teaspoon fresh lemon juice, or to taste
Salt and freshly ground white pepper to taste

1.   Bring a large saucepan of salted water to a boil. Meanwhile, combine the butter and cayenne in another saucepan and place over a low heat to melt the butter; keep warm.
2.   Rinse the Brussels sprouts well, discarding any blemished ones. Slice off and discard the root ends. Then cut each sprout into three or four slices. (Use a sharp knife, not a shredder, which would cut them too thin.)
3.   Add the sprouts to the boiling water and cook no more than 2 to 3 minutes. Drain at once and toss with the melted butter and cayenne. Add the lemon juice, season with salt and white pepper, and serve immediately.

Serves 6

You can slice the sprouts a day ahead, if you like. Cover and refrigerate until you're ready to cook them.

Do not use a shredder, as it cuts the sprouts too thin and they will not retain their texture.

## WINTER VEGETABLES FOR CHRISTMASTIME

Acorn squash
Cauliflower
Celery
Cabbage, red and green
Celeriac (also known as celery root)
Sweet potatoes
White potatoes

Salsify
Parsnips
Broccoli
Zucchini
Green beans
Lettuces

## FOUR-STAR CORNMEAL BUTTERFLAKE BISCUITS

I thought there would never be a biscuit to challenge the traditional Southern buttermilk biscuit, but here it is. This will become a standby for you, as it has for me—a dyed-in-the-wool biscuit lover takes a bow! These biscuits freeze superbly and taste freshly baked when reheated—unbelievable. They will become a lifelong friend.

1 package dry yeast
¼ cup warm water
2½ cups all-purpose flour (measured before sifting)
½ cup (1 stick) unsalted butter, chilled and cut into small pieces
2 teaspoons sugar
1½ teaspoons salt
¾ cup finely ground white cornmeal
1 large egg
¾ cup cold milk
4 tablespoons (½ stick) unsalted butter, melted

1.  Combine the yeast and the warm water in a small bowl and stir to dissolve the yeast. Set it aside.
2.  Sift the flour into a large mixing bowl and gradually add the butter, cutting it in with a pastry blender until it is finely crumbled. (Do not use a food processor for this.) Add the sugar, salt, and cornmeal. Mix thoroughly.
3.  Stir the egg and the dissolved yeast into the flour mixture and mix well. Then add the milk and mix again, but don't overmix. Keep the dough light.
4.  Toss the dough onto a lightly floured surface and knead it very gently for a minute or two. If it is too sticky to handle, add a few extra tablespoons of cornmeal. The dough should be soft and malleable.
5.  Place the dough in a greased bowl and turn it to coat all sides. Cover the bowl with plastic wrap and set it in a warm place for the dough to rise until doubled in bulk, about 45 to 50 minutes, but the time will vary with the heat of the kitchen.
6.  Punch down the dough. (If you like, at this point you can wrap the dough in plastic and refrigerate it for up to 2 days.)
7.  Preheat the oven to 425°F.
8.  Return the dough to a lightly floured surface and knead it lightly. Roll it out to a thickness of ⅛ inch (yes, paper-thin) and cut it into 2-inch biscuits.

9.  Brush half of the biscuits with melted butter and place the unbuttered biscuits on top of the buttered ones. Then butter the tops of those biscuits. Cover lightly with plastic wrap and set in a warm place to rise until they spring back when lightly touched, about 25 to 30 minutes.

10. Bake the biscuits on the middle rack of the preheated oven until golden brown, 18 to 20 minutes. Serve at once.

Makes 25 to 30 biscuits

VARIATION:
You can separate the biscuits after baking and insert cooked ham or bacon between the layers, then quickly reheat—an exquisite Christmas biscuit!

To freeze the cooked biscuits, let them cool completely. Then seal them in plastic bags and freeze. To reheat, brush them with additional butter if you like (it's not necessary) and bake for 6 to 8 minutes in a preheated 400°F oven.

Stone-ground and yellow cornmeals have their place—but not in this recipe. Use finely ground white cornmeal only, please.

## KENTUCKY EGGNOG ICE CREAM

The nuance of flavors in this Eggnog Ice Cream—created by blending bourbon and brandy—is the touchstone of its charm. This is an exquisite holiday dessert—refreshing after Christmas dinner, fun for a fireside picnic, and beguiling at a midnight New Year's supper. A small scoop, garnished with a fresh or candied violet, in a crystal dish, is lovely for a Christmas tea.

The variation is a treasure within itself, but for Christmas my choice is the standard Eggnog Ice Cream.

6 large egg yolks
¾ cup sugar
2 cups whole milk
Tiny pinch of salt
1 teaspoon cognac vanilla (see page 29) or pure vanilla extract
1 quart heavy or whipping cream, cold
1 cup best-quality bourbon
½ cup cognac or brandy

1.  Place a large bowl, stainless steel if possible, in the refrigerator to chill.
2.  Using an electric mixer, beat the egg yolks and sugar together in a large mixing bowl until the mixture turns a lighter shade of yellow and the texture is creamy.
3.  Whisk the milk into the egg mixture. Pour the mixture into a heavy 1½- to 2-quart saucepan and cook over a medium heat until the custard coats a wooden spoon nicely.
4.  Immediately pour the custard into the chilled bowl, cover it with plastic wrap, and refrigerate it until thoroughly chilled, about 1 hour (taste it to check).
5.  When you are ready to make the ice cream, stir in the salt, cognac vanilla, cream, bourbon, and cognac. Freeze in an ice-cream maker according to the manufacturer's directions.

Makes 1¼ gallons

VARIATION:
Grand Marnier Ice Cream: Omit the bourbon and cognac; instead, add ½ cup Grand Marnier. Freeze as directed.

The rich custard is one of the secrets here. If you want a lighter ice cream, cook the custard less, so that it coats the wooden spoon very lightly or not at all. But don't cut corners on the ingredients. Use whole milk and heavy cream, and the best bourbon and cognac.

## MOTHER'S AMBROSIA

This was Mother's favorite Christmas dessert, and the entire family loved it as well. It is gloriously light and refreshing, a delightful finale for an otherwise rich meal. Oftentimes, however, Mother would serve a pumpkin pie too!

*9 to 11 navel oranges*
*Sugar to taste*
*1 fresh coconut, grated, or 1 package grated coconut*

1. Peel the oranges, removing any white pith that remains. Cut the fruit into sections and place them in a serving bowl. Add sugar if it is needed. Cover and chill in the refrigerator until you are ready to serve.
2. Spoon the oranges into individual dessert bowls or into a large crystal bowl and spoon coconut over the top. Serve immediately.

Serves 6 to 8

## PLUM PUDDING PIE

This is one of the most delectable mélanges of winter holiday fruits I know. It says "Christmas" with all its heart.

*1 cup black seedless raisins*
*1 cup dried currants*
*½ cup pitted prunes, halved or slivered*
*2 ounces candied orange, finely chopped*
*2 ounces candied lemon, finely chopped*
*2 ounces candied citron, finely chopped*

⅓ cup good-quality bourbon or brandy
1 cup sugar
Zest of 1 lemon
Zest of 1 navel orange
8 ounces beef kidney suet, ground (see owl, next page)
1 teaspoon cognac vanilla (see page 29)
1½ teaspoons ground cinnamon
½ teaspoon ground allspice
½ teaspoon ground coriander
¼ teaspoon ground cloves
¼ teaspoon freshly grated nutmeg
5 large eggs, lightly beaten
½ cup soft fresh bread crumbs
Flaky Butter Pastry dough for a 10-inch 2-crust pie (see page 50)
¼ cup milk, or heavy or whipping cream, to coat the pastry (optional)
Whipped cream flavored with brandy or cognac, for serving

1. Combine the raisins, currants, prunes, and candied fruits in a mixing bowl and pour the bourbon over them. Cover and marinate for a few hours or as long as overnight.
2. Preheat the oven to 425°F.
3. Combine the sugar, lemon zest, and orange zest in a food processor and twirl until the zest is finely grated (or grate the zest by hand and add to the sugar). Pour the sugar mixture into a large mixing bowl.
4. Add the suet to the sugar and mix well. Add the marinated fruits, cognac vanilla, spices, eggs, and bread crumbs. Blend thoroughly by hand so the fruits will not be mashed.
5. Line a 10-inch ovenproof glass pie plate with half the pastry dough and cut the rest of the dough into lattice strips. Spoon the fruit mixture into the pie plate, filling it no more than ¾ full. Cover with the lattice strips, crimp the top and bottom edges together, and trim evenly with the rim of the plate. Brush the lattice strips with milk or cream, which gives a flaky and shiny crust.

6. Bake the pie on the lowest rack of the preheated oven for about 45 minutes. Watch it carefully. If the crust starts to brown too quickly, cover it loosely with foil and reduce the heat to 375°F.
7. Serve warm or at room temperature with flavored whipped cream.

Serves 10

 Ask your butcher to grind the beef kidney suet, or if you have a food processor, use that to grind it.

It bears repeating that the suet from around the kidney is the best, as it is less fibrous and stringy.

## CHOCOLATE ALMOND TOFFEE

Toffee is one of the best homemade candies I know—and Christmas isn't Christmas without candy, is it? This toffee is delicious plain, but the coating of chocolate makes it especially marvelous.

*1½ cups whole almonds, blanched or unblanched*
*1 cup (2 sticks) unsalted butter*
*1¼ cups sugar*
*3 tablespoons light corn syrup*
*¼ teaspoon cream of tartar*
*Pinch of salt*
*2 teaspoons pure vanilla extract, cognac vanilla (see page 29), or brandy*
*4 or 5 ounces semisweet chocolate, melted (see owl, next page)*

1. Preheat the oven to 160°F.
2. Spread the almonds on a rimmed pastry sheet and bake them in the preheated oven until they are dry and crisp, about 2 hours. Watch them carefully—you don't want to toast them. Set them aside, still on the pastry sheet.

3. Combine the butter, sugar, corn syrup, cream of tartar, and salt in a heavy 2-quart (or larger) saucepan and bring to a boil. Cover the pan and let the mixture cook for 3 to 4 minutes, allowing the steam to dissolve the sugar crystals that form on the sides of the pan. Remove the cover and continue to cook, stirring gently, until the syrup registers 300°F on a candy thermometer, about 3 to 4 minutes after it reaches the boiling point (watch it carefully). As it cooks, keep wiping the sides of the pan with a pastry brush that has been dipped in boiling water (or better still, in melted butter) to remove the sugar crystals. If at any time the toffee seems to be darkening too fast, place the pan over a flame tamer to keep the toffee from burning.

4. Remove the toffee from the heat, allow the boiling to subside for a second or two, then stir in the vanilla.

5. Pour the toffee over the almonds on the pastry sheet, stirring to cover them thoroughly with the syrup and to spread the mixture evenly over the sheet. Allow the toffee to cool.

6. When the toffee has set, brush it with the melted chocolate. Let the chocolate cool and solidify and then break the candy into jagged pieces. Store it in an airtight tin.

Makes about 1½ pounds

Chocolate should always be melted over simmering (never boiling) water, and it won't tolerate a single drop of water or even steam, which will cause the chocolate to be lumpy.

## MENU 10

Champagne, Chilled White Wine, or Red Wine
*Oysters in Scallop Shells*
*Roast Quail with Tarragon*
*Madras Chutney with Almonds*
*Bibb, Endive, and Walnut Salad*
*Mother's Dinner Rolls*
*Mincemeat Pie*
Demitasse

As the autumn leaves began to fade and winter's chilly days came along, the wild ducks would quack their way in the night flying south. It was an eerie sound, but we knew it meant that Christmas was on its way. My father was a huntsman and a fisherman when he was younger. We were poor but we had good food. The farmers would bring their wild catch to our little hotel to sell. Mother was a wonderful cook and we dined rather gloriously. There was not much grouse, but bobwhite quails abounded and they were my favorite. Mother cooked them to a perfect golden brown, crisp and succulent—and with her hot rolls and biscuits, nothing could be more delicious. These memories inspired one of the best Christmas dinners I know. Mother didn't use tarragon with the quail, as the herb was not well known at that time, but it blends with the quail as no other herb does.

## OYSTERS IN SCALLOP SHELLS

From the Chesapeake Bay to New Orleans, oysters are one of the South's favorite seafoods. They make a perfect first course or hors d'oeuvre, as they are light and flavorful—the very definition of an appetizer.

6 tablespoons (¾ stick) unsalted butter
1 pound fresh mushrooms, sliced
½ cup red bell pepper, finely chopped
1 pint shucked fresh oysters
2 tablespoons water
1 or 2 shallots, peeled and finely chopped
1½ tablespoons all-purpose flour
1 cup heavy or whipping cream
1 tablespoon medium-dry Spanish sherry or Madeira, or more to taste
Salt and freshly ground white pepper to taste
Cayenne pepper to taste
¼ teaspoon ground mace
1½ cups buttered and toasted bread crumbs
Chopped fresh parsley, for garnish

1. Melt 3 tablespoons of the butter in a heavy nonstick skillet and sauté the mushrooms and red bell pepper in it until just tender, about 3 minutes (no longer, as they must remain somewhat crisp). Set aside.
2. Drain the oysters. Using sharp, thin scissors, cut the oysters in half, or in thirds if they're very large. Set them aside.
3. Combine 1 tablespoon of the butter with the water in a skillet and sauté the shallots until they are limp but not brown, 1 to 2 minutes. Stir in the remaining 2 tablespoons butter with the flour and blend. Add the cream and simmer until the roux has thickened, stirring constantly.
4. In another pan, heat the oysters over a low heat until they begin to curl. Drain them, reserving the liquid.
5. Add the oysters and the sautéed mushrooms and bell pepper to the roux. If the mixture is too thick, thin it with some of the reserved oyster liquid (not with more cream). Season with the sherry, salt, white pepper, cayenne, and mace.
6. Heat the mixture, but *do not allow it to boil*. Spoon it into tiny scallop shells, sprinkle with the bread crumbs and parsley, and serve at once.

Serves 6 to 8

The size of the scallop shells will determine the exact number of servings.

### ABOUT OYSTERS

The oyster is a lazy little mollusk. Snuggled tightly in a brownish gray shell, it lies in bed all day and night. It never struggles for food and hobnobs only with the tiny crab that attaches itself inside the oyster's pearly coat.

All this tranquility makes the oyster the most tender and succulent of all seafoods. It rests in our tummies as quietly as it hides in the dark coves of rocky, salty waters; nothing could be easier to digest. Dr. Johnson said of oysters: "They nourish wonderfully, and solicit rest."

## Roast Quail with Tarragon

For this Christmas menu, quail is the bird of choice, but if unavailable, substitute tiny one-pound chickens (*poussins* in French) or even very small chicken breasts, cut in half. (The larding and seasonings will remain the same.) Allow two quail per guest and two extra for the platter, for the sake of hospitality (but really for your lunch the next day—nothing is more delicious than cold quail).

*14 quail, thawed if frozen*
*10 tablespoons unsalted butter, at room temperature*
*1 tablespoon chopped fresh tarragon leaves, or 1½ teaspoons dried tarragon*
*1 tablespoon chopped fresh parsley*
*Salt to taste*
*14 teaspoons Spanish sherry or Madeira*
*14 slices smoked bacon*
*Freshly ground white pepper to taste*
*Cayenne pepper to taste*
*1¼ cups homemade chicken stock*
*1 tablespoon Spanish sherry or Madeira, for the sauce (optional)*

1. Preheat the oven to 475°F. Rinse the quail and dry them thoroughly with paper towels.
2. In a small bowl, blend together the butter, tarragon, and parsley until smooth. Season lightly with salt.
3. Spoon 1 teaspoon sherry into the cavity of each quail, along with a dab of the seasoned butter. Wrap a strip of bacon firmly around each bird (cut the slices in half if they're too long) and secure it with a toothpick.
4. Place the quail in a shallow roasting pan and bake on the middle rack of the preheated oven for about 20 to 25 minutes.
5. Remove the bacon, sprinkle the quail with white pepper and cayenne, and return them to the oven for about 5 minutes or until golden brown and tender when stuck with a cooking fork. Transfer the quail to a heated serving platter and pour the pan juices into a small saucepan. Stir the stock into the pan juices and bring the mixture to a simmer. Add a tablespoon of sherry if you like. Serve the sauce at the table.

Serves 6 or 7

## Madras Chutney with Almonds

Chutney is an Indian condiment that traditionally accompanies curry dishes. When the British occupied India, curries and chutneys became an integral part of their cuisine, and during the American colonial period the English passed them on to us. We did not readily accept curries in the South, but we made chutneys like mad. The Indian chutney made of mangoes remains the finest. Mangoes are plentiful in Florida and California, so we can make superb Indian chutneys—and the recipe given here is for one of the best. The mangoes should be green so they retain some texture.

8 pounds green mangoes, peeled and cut into large slices
½ pound fresh ginger root, peeled and cut into thin slivers
1 small Vidalia onion, peeled and thinly sliced
¼ pound sultana (golden) raisins
Juice of 2 lemons
2 tablespoons pure (uniodized) salt
1 tablespoon cayenne pepper
3 cinnamon sticks (3 to 4 inches long), broken in half
3 imported bay leaves
1 quart cider vinegar
3½ pounds sugar
3 tablespoons fresh lime juice
1½ cups whole blanched almonds

1.  Combine all the ingredients except the sugar, lime juice, and almonds in a large stainless-steel kettle. Stir thoroughly. Let the mixture stand, covered, for 3 hours in a cool place or overnight in the refrigerator.
2.  Bring the mixture to a boil and simmer until the mango and onion are just barely tender, about 1 hour. Do not let the mango slices get too soft.
3.  Stir in the sugar and lime juice and cook over a moderate heat until the syrup is thick, 2 to 2½ hours. Watch the chutney carefully and stir it frequently while it is cooking. When it is ready, stir in the almonds.
4.  Pour the hot chutney into hot sterilized pint jars and seal at once if they will be processed (place jars in a boiling water bath for 5 minutes) for shelf storage. The jars do not have to be processed if you are going to store them in the refrigerator or freezer; simply allow the jars to cool before placing them in the refrigerator or freezer. (Freezing is the best method, as it retains that "just made" flavor.)

Makes about 8 pints

VARIATION:
If you like, add 1 or 2 peeled whole garlic cloves about 30 minutes before the chutney is done. Don't overdo the garlic, however—the other flavors are too delicious to be disguised.

## BIBB, ENDIVE, AND WALNUT SALAD

This is one of the most festive and delicious salads I know, and many friends and students have agreed.

6 heads Bibb lettuce
2 heads Belgian endive
1 cup large walnut pieces
1 tablespoon unsalted butter
1½ tablespoons sugar
Cayenne pepper to taste
3 tablespoons Worcestershire sauce
6 tablespoons walnut oil
3 tablespoons champagne vinegar
Salt to taste
Dash of fresh lemon juice

1. Rinse and dry the greens. Store them in the refrigerator.
2. Pick over the walnuts, discarding any crumbs. Melt the butter in a small skillet, add the walnuts, and stir over a low heat until they are well coated and fairly crisp, about 2 minutes. Stir in the sugar and cayenne. Mix thoroughly. Add the Worcestershire sauce and continue to stir until the walnuts have a thin dark glaze, about 2 minutes. Set them aside.
3. Stir together the walnut oil, vinegar, salt, and lemon juice. Set the dressing aside.
4. When you are ready to serve the salad, arrange the Bibb lettuce leaves in a shallow bowl. Cut the endive into slivers and sprinkle them over the lettuce. Spoon the walnuts into the center and top with the dressing.

Serves 4

## MOTHER'S DINNER ROLLS

When making these yeast rolls over the years (and I have made hundreds), many times a picture has come to mind of our old-fashioned kitchen at our little hotel and of Mother making up the dough the night before, placing it in a large stone bowl, covering it with a clean porous cloth, and placing it on a high shelf for overnight rising. The next day she would punch down the dough and add a little flour if it seemed overly sticky. She would then cover the dough again and put it in the refrigerator (which was called an icebox in those days) to chill. An hour or so before dinner, Mother would shape the dough into rolls and allow them to double in bulk. Then they were baked fresh for dinner.

*1 package dry yeast*
*¼ cup lukewarm water*
*4½ cups sifted all-purpose flour*
*3 tablespoons sugar*
*1 teaspoon salt*
*3 tablespoons solid vegetable shortening, chilled*
*1½ cups buttermilk*
*3 tablespoons unsalted butter, melted, plus more for brushing if desired*

1. In a small bowl, dissolve the yeast in the water.
2. Sift the flour, sugar, and salt into a large bowl. Cut in the shortening using a pastry blender. Add the dissolved yeast and buttermilk and mix the dough thoroughly with a wooden spoon.
3. Toss the dough onto a well-floured surface and knead for a few seconds. The dough should be soft and sticky. Place the dough in a lightly greased bowl and turn to grease all sides. Cover the bowl with plastic wrap and put it in a warm, draft-free place for the dough to rise until doubled in bulk, about 1 hour.

4.  Turn out the dough on a lightly floured surface. Roll it into a 22 × 14-inch rectangle about ¼ inch thick. With a 2-inch biscuit cutter, cut out about 40 rounds, or as many as you can. Don't reroll the scraps.

5.  Lightly dip each side of the rounds into the melted butter. Fold 2 opposite edges of each round into the center and pinch together firmly. Arrange the rolls side by side in rows on a lightly greased baking sheet; they should be touching to prevent them from springing open.

6.  Cover the rolls lightly with plastic wrap and set them aside in a warm place until doubled in bulk, about 45 minutes.

7.  Preheat the oven to 400°F. Bake the rolls on the middle rack of the preheated oven for 5 minutes, then lower the heat to 375°F and bake until light golden brown, 15 to 20 minutes longer. For soft, buttery rolls, brush them with melted butter as soon as they come out of the oven. Serve at once.

Makes about 40 rolls

When the dough is made the night before and allowed to rise at room temperature, it ferments just a little, and this adds a dimension of flavor.

The cooked rolls can be cooled, wrapped in foil, and set aside overnight. Rewarm before serving.

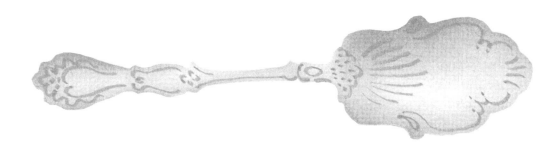

## MINCEMEAT PIE

Time doesn't go by fast at all—think of mincemeat, for instance. We make it now for Christmas pies and cookies, and it tastes fresh and delicious and better than ever, yet the recipe is hundreds of years old and hasn't changed as much as one might think.

More than three hundred years ago—on December 25, 1666, sixty years before Jamestown, Virginia, was settled—Samuel Pepys, the famous English diarist, wrote: "Lay pretty long in bed, and then rose, leaving my wife desirous to sleep, having sat up 'till four this morning seeing her maid make mince pyes."

*2½ to 3 cups mincemeat*
*½ cup chopped peeled apples*
*½ cup chopped walnuts*
*¼ cup cognac or brandy, or 2 tablespoons Jamaica rum plus 2 tablespoons bourbon*
*Standard or Flaky Butter Pastry dough for a 2-crust pie (see page 48 or 52)*
*Cream or milk for brushing the crust*

1. Combine the mincemeat, apples, walnuts, and cognac in a large bowl and set aside, covered, to marinate for a few hours or as long as overnight.
2. Preheat the oven to 425°F.
3. Roll out half the pastry dough and fit it into a 9- or 10-inch pie plate (glass is best). Leave a 1-inch overhang.
4. Spoon the mincemeat mixture into the crust, filling it no more than ¾ full.
5. Roll out the remaining dough to form an 11-inch circle. Place it over the mincemeat, folding the edge of the top crust under the edge of the bottom crust, trimming as necessary to keep the edges from being too bulky. Crimp the edges together. Cut some slits in the top crust for air vents (this is important—don't skip it).
6. Brush the top and edges of the crust with cream or milk to give it a glaze (cream or milk makes it shiny and flaky).

7. Place the pie on the bottom rack of the preheated oven and bake until the crust is golden brown, about 45 minutes. If the top browns too quickly, reduce the heat to 375° F and cover the pie loosely with foil.
8. Let the pie cool a bit before serving; it is good warm, but not hot.

Serves 8

When the bottom crust is nicely browned, the pie is usually done. That's one advantage of a glass pie plate—you can actually see the bottom of the pie as it bakes.

To save time, roll out the crusts a day or two ahead. Place them on a foil-lined pastry sheet with more aluminum foil between the layers. Wrap the entire package in foil and freeze it. Thaw before baking.

## THE JOY OF MINCEMEAT

Mincemeat goes back a long way. We inherited the idea from England, our mother country, but culinary historians believe it was first made by the Romans. We do know that "Minst Pye" was made in Elizabethan England, for it appears in *The Good Hous-Wives Treasurie*, published in 1588, and the recipe is similar to the ones we use today.

In old England, when a ship loaded with a cargo of sweet-smelling spices arrived at the East Dock in London, there was much rejoicing. Spices were very dear at the time and represented a luxury. That is the reason, no doubt, why pies and puddings redolent with spices were reserved for celebrations and holidays in the early days of our country.

Mincemeat is as delicious as ever, and your own homemade variety is the very best, a real treat for everyone. A number of different sweetmeats can be made, to be used for pies, cakes, tarts, and turnovers.

Christmas in the South would not be Christmas without mincemeat!

## MENU II

Champagne, Chilled White Wine, or Red Wine
*Pork Loin Roast with Cider and Mother's Poached Apples*
*Carolina Potato Rolls*
Buttered Broccoli
Mashed Potatoes
*Tangerine Pie*
*Castlewood Pumpkin or Persimmon Cake*
*with Cream Cheese Frosting*
*Kentucky Bourbon Balls*
Coffee

The pig is a very gracious fellow. He is always in a good humor—his grunt is just his native language. He can live in the house with you, as he does in Denmark, or he can live in a pen on your farm, large or small.

The pig's meat tastes good from his head to his tail, and every cut can be cooked in many different ways.

The Southern states, all the way through Maryland, Virginia, Kentucky, Tennessee, and North Carolina, are very partial to the pig. Kentucky and Virginia are the most famous for curing the hams of the pig; in fact, it is on record that Queen Victoria of England even ordered country hams from Virginia.

Pigs adore peanuts and corn and they are never happier than when they are free to dine in an orchard of windfall apples. Their meat has a great affinity for apples, too; in fact, hams that are smoked over apple wood are considered the best.

We may live without
  poetry, music and art;
We may live without con-
  science, and live without
  heart;
We may live without
  friends; we may live
  without books;
But civilized man cannot
  live without cooks.

—Edward Robert
  Bulwer-Lytton

We are very fond of fresh pork in the South. The loin is the most expensive cut. It is probably at its best when served with poached apples. The loin, cooked with apple cider for special occasions like Christmas, is as delectable as it is festive.

Serve the loin of pork hot, garnished with watercress as well as poached apples, or make it into sandwiches the next day. All kinds of mustard are wonderful with these sandwiches, and one of the best is Rothchild's Red Raspberry Mustard, made in Urbana, Ohio, at Robert Rothchild's berry farm. Try to find it.

# PORK LOIN ROAST WITH CIDER AND MOTHER'S POACHED APPLES

**A**sk your butcher to cut through the chine bone; it should remain loosely attached to render its flavor to the roast, but then it can be removed for easier carving when the roast is done.

*2 teaspoons salt*
*1 teaspoon dried rosemary, crumbled*
*4- to 5-pound center-cut pork loin roast*
*½ cup homemade chicken stock*
*1 cup apple cider*
*Freshly ground white pepper to taste*
*Watercress sprigs, for garnish*
*Mother's Poached Apples (recipe follows), for garnish*

1. Preheat the oven to 325°F.
2. Stir the salt and rosemary together and rub the mixture thoroughly over the pork roast. Place the roast, fat side up, on a rack in a large roasting pan. Cook for 35 minutes per pound: 2 hours and 20 minutes for a 4-pound roast, 2 hours and 55 minutes for a 5-pound roast.
3. Halfway through the roasting time, pour the chicken stock and cider over the roast and sprinkle the white pepper over it. The roast is done when it registers 160°F on an instant-reading thermometer.
4. Transfer the roast to a wooden carving board or a warm platter and garnish it with watercress and poached apples.

Serves 8 to 10

# MOTHER'S POACHED APPLES

*8 to 10 small apples, such as Granny Smith, Rome Beauty,*
*    or Golden Delicious*
*2 cups water*
*3 slices lemon*
*¾ cup sugar, or to taste*
*1 cup apple jelly*

1.  Peel and core the apples, but leave them whole.
2.  Combine the water, lemon slices, and sugar in a deep, heavy pan. Add the apples. Bring to a low boil and cook, basting the apples almost constantly, until they are tender but have not lost their shape, about 30 minutes.
3.  Transfer the apples to a platter and, while they are cooling, fill the cavities with the apple jelly.

# CAROLINA POTATO ROLLS

Potatoes are far more versatile than one might think. Among their many uses, they are rather magical in making a variety of breads, sweet and savory—especially yeast breads, but even quick breads that are leavened with baking powder.

The potato lends a soft, close-grained texture and a special moistness to the unbaked yeast dough. One half cup unseasoned mashed potatoes can be substituted for ½ cup flour in any yeast bread recipe.

The potato breads are among the favorites of my students and their families, and of my own family, of course, as well. There are few aromas more appetizing than homemade bread baking away in our ovens. It makes us so hungry we can hardly wait.

1 package dry yeast
¼ cup lukewarm water
½ cup freshly cooked mashed potatoes, sieved or riced, hot
⅓ cup unsalted butter, at room temperature
3 tablespoons sugar
1¼ teaspoons salt
1 large egg
½ cup milk, lukewarm to warm
3 cups sifted all-purpose flour
3 tablespoons unsalted butter, melted
2 to 3 tablespoons poppy seeds, for topping (optional)

1.  Combine the yeast and lukewarm water in a small bowl and stir to dissolve the yeast. Set aside.
2.  Put the hot mashed potatoes in a large bowl and add the ⅓ cup butter, stirring to melt it. Add the sugar, salt, egg, and dissolved yeast and beat thoroughly.
3.  Alternately add the milk and flour to the potato mixture in small amounts, beating thoroughly.
4.  Transfer the dough to a lightly floured surface and knead it thoroughly. Add a little flour if needed to keep the dough from being too sticky.
5.  Place the dough in a lightly greased bowl and turn it to coat all sides. Cover the bowl with plastic wrap and place in a warm spot for the dough to rise until doubled in bulk, about 1 hour.
6.  Meanwhile, lightly grease 2 pastry sheets and lightly dust them with flour (or you can use nonstick sheets).

7.   When the dough has doubled in bulk, punch it down and place it on a lightly floured surface. Divide it into two parts, and refrigerate one portion. Roll out the other half until it is ¼ inch thick. Cut the rolls with a round 2½-inch biscuit cutter; cut out as many rounds as you can (about 15). Dip one side of each round in the melted butter, then fold over, with the butter on the inside, like a pocketbook roll. Place the rolls, barely touching one another, on one of the prepared pastry sheets (if the rolls do not touch, they are likely to spring open). Sprinkle them with poppy seeds if you like. Repeat with the other half of the dough.

8.   Cover both pastry sheets with plastic wrap and set in a warm place until the rolls have doubled in bulk, about 1 hour.

9.   Meanwhile, preheat the oven to 375°F.

10.   Bake the rolls on the middle rack of the preheated oven until they are golden brown, about 18 minutes. Serve at once.

Makes about 30 rolls

 Potatoes make a very moist product when they're added to almost any dough. They're also flavorful and nutritious!

You can let the baked rolls cool, then wrap them in aluminum foil and freeze them for up to 1 week. When you're ready to use them, place the rolls, frozen or thawed, in a preheated 350°F oven and bake for 25 to 30 minutes or until beautifully browned.

## TANGERINE PIE

The tangerine is an especially delicious type of orange that comes in season during the winter, which makes it a special treat in December. The tangerine, like the other oranges and the lemon, is native to China, but that was in the long ago—thousands of years ago, in fact. The name tangerine is derived from the city of Tangier in North Africa, where the fruit is widely grown.

The Temple orange is a hybrid of the mandarin orange (another name for the tangerine). The Clementine and the Satsuma are closely related to them. All these oranges are sweet in flavor and are a joy of the Christmas season. One of their great charms is that the skins slip off very easily by hand and do not have to be peeled, and any of them can be used in this recipe.

This pie is both charming and flavorful. The crust can be made ahead of time, but I suggest you use the filling immediately after preparing it.

### PIE FILLING
⅓ cup sugar
Zest of ½ lemon
Zest of 2 tangerines (see owl, next page)
1 tablespoon arrowroot
3 large eggs, separated
1 whole large egg
⅓ cup fresh tangerine juice
1 tablespoon fresh lemon juice
1 tablespoon heavy or whipping cream
Pinch of salt
6 tablespoons unsalted butter, chilled and cut into small pieces
Flaky Butter Pastry for a 9-inch 1-crust pie (see page 50),
    baked and chilled

### MERINGUE
4 large egg whites
½ cup sugar

1. Place a medium-size stainless-steel bowl in the refrigerator to chill.
2. Combine the sugar, lemon zest, and tangerine zest in a food processor and twirl until the zest is finely grated. (You can grate the citrus zest by hand and add it to the sugar, but the processor does a wonderful job and is easier.)

3. Add the arrowroot to the sugar mixture. Mix thoroughly. Combine with the 3 egg yolks and 1 whole egg in a heavy saucepan. Beat thoroughly with a whisk.

4. Add the tangerine juice, lemon juice, cream, and salt to the egg and sugar mixture. Place the mixture over a medium heat and beat constantly, stirring in one direction only. Add the small pieces of butter, a few at a time (this thickens the custard more effectively than adding all the butter at once). Do not stop stirring. The custard will thicken quickly; watch it carefully. When the custard coats a wooden spoon heavily, it is done. Remove from the heat and pour at once into the chilled stainless-steel bowl (this stops the custard from cooking anymore). Cover the bowl with plastic wrap and refrigerate until the custard has chilled. (This tangerine custard, well covered or in a tightly sealed clean jar, will keep for several days in the refrigerator.)

5. When ready to bake the pie, preheat the oven to 350°F.

6. Spoon the custard evenly into the baked and chilled pie crust.

7. For the meringue, whip the egg whites until they form soft peaks. Add the sugar slowly, beating constantly until the meringue forms stiff peaks. Spread the meringue evenly over the custard, making certain it completely covers the custard.

8. Place the pie on the middle rack of the preheated oven and bake until the meringue is a very light golden color, about 15 minutes. Serve at room temperature or chilled.

Serves 8

VARIATION:
*Lemon Pie:* Substitute lemon zest and lemon juice for the tangerine zest and juice. Additional sugar will probably be needed; add to your taste.

Tangerine zest can be difficult to grate. If desired, the zest from navel or Temple oranges or from tangelos can be used instead. As for the juice, though, nothing is so special as fresh tangerine juice.

## ABOUT CORNSTARCH AND ARROWROOT

Cornstarch is used for thickening sauces and puddings. It has twice the thickening power of flour, but unlike flour, when it cooks it is transparent and rather glossy. It is more tedious to deal with than flour, however, as it will break if overbeaten.

Arrowroot is the best thickening agent of all for very special fruit pastries, pies, and so on, but it is so expensive that it cannot be used commercially, or even used widely in the home kitchen. Arrowroot is absolutely flavorless and it thickens beautifully.

# CASTLEWOOD PUMPKIN OR PERSIMMON CAKE WITH CREAM CHEESE FROSTING

After the first frost, wild persimmons will be ripe and can be substituted for the pumpkin in this cake. Either cake makes a delicious spicy country dessert served with coffee on a wintry night. The cakes are also good for tea and a minute of rest from a busy day of Christmas shopping.

The cakes freeze well, to be eaten later with one of your holiday meals. I do not know a more delicious pumpkin or persimmon cake.

*½ cup (1 stick) unsalted butter, at room temperature*
*1½ cups granulated or light brown sugar, or a mixture of both*
*2 large eggs*
*1¾ cups sifted all-purpose flour*
*¾ teaspoon salt*
*1¾ teaspoons baking powder*

¾ teaspoon baking soda
1½ teaspoons ground cinnamon
½ teaspoon ground allspice
½ teaspoon ground coriander
½ teaspoon freshly grated
    nutmeg
¼ teaspoon ground cloves
1 cup freshly cooked pump-
    kin, strained; canned
    puréed pumpkin; or lightly
    cooked puréed ripe
    persimmons
⅓ cup water
1 teaspoon cognac vanilla
    (see page 29)
½ cup coarsely chopped
    pecans or walnuts (optional)
Cream Cheese Frosting
    (recipe follows) or
    confectioners' sugar

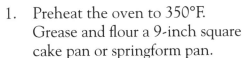

1.  Preheat the oven to 350°F.
    Grease and flour a 9-inch square
    cake pan or springform pan.
2.  Cream the butter and sugar thoroughly with an electric mixer. Add the
    eggs and continue to beat hard until the mixture changes to a lighter shade
    of yellow and has increased in volume.
3.  Sift the flour, salt, baking powder, baking soda, and spices together into a
    large mixing bowl.
4.  Combine the pumpkin and water in a small bowl. Using a whisk or a
    wooden spoon, alternately add the pumpkin and the flour to the egg mix-
    ture, mixing well. Fold in the vanilla and the nuts (if you are using
    them).
5.  Pour the batter into the prepared pan, place it on the middle rack of the

preheated oven, and bake until the cake springs back at once when lightly touched, about 35 minutes.

6.   Remove the cake from the oven and let it stand for a few minutes in the pan. Then loosen the sides of the cake with a thin knife and turn it out on a wire rack to cool.

7.   Ice the cooled cake with Cream Cheese Frosting or dust it with sifted confectioners' sugar.

Serves 6 to 8

VARIATION:
If you like, add a touch of lemon or orange juice and grated zest to the batter.

You can bake this cake in a standard-size loaf pan. Allow 1 hour baking time.

## CREAM CHEESE FROSTING

¼ pound cream cheese, at room temperature
3 tablespoons unsalted butter, at room temperature
1½ cups sifted confectioners' sugar
1 teaspoon cognac vanilla (see page 29)

Combine the cream cheese and butter in a food processor or with an electric mixer and process until well blended. Add the confectioners' sugar and cognac vanilla and process until smooth. Chill, covered, in the refrigerator until it has a good spreading consistency, 30 minutes to 1 hour.

## KENTUCKY BOURBON BALLS

This yummy chocolate confection, half cake, half candy, is believed to have been created in Kentucky by a German immigrant. It is impossible to unravel these culinary mysteries, but this I know: the recipe traveled fast because it is both delightful and easy to make. It's best when made with leftover homemade cake, but vanilla wafers work fine, too.

1 cup leftover white cake or vanilla wafer crumbs
1 cup sifted confectioners' sugar
¼ cup unsweetened cocoa powder, or to taste
3 tablespoons light corn syrup
¼ cup bourbon
1 cup chopped pecans
Unsweetened cocoa powder, for coating

1. Combine the crumbs, confectioners' sugar, ¼ cup cocoa powder, corn syrup, and bourbon in a food processor or with an electric mixer. Blend until thoroughly mixed. Using a spoon, stir in the pecans.
2. Roll tablespoonfuls of the mixture to form small truffle-size balls. (The mixture should be soft. If it is too dry to roll easily, add a little more corn syrup.)
3. Spread cocoa powder on a plate and roll the balls in it to coat them. Store the bourbon balls in an airtight tin and refrigerate them (or you can freeze them).

Makes 30 to 36 balls

# An Elegant Christmas Dinner

## Menu 12

Champagne

Olives

*Roquefort-Stuffed Celery Curls*

Beluga Caviar

Shrimp

*Marinated Beef Tenderloin with Old English Walnut Sauce*

*Wild Rice*

*Velvet Crumb Rolls*

*Bibb Lettuce, Endive, and Spiced Walnut Salad*

*Tangerine Sherbet*

*Winter Crystal Cookies*

Demitasse

One of my students asked me one year to design an elegant Christmas dinner menu that could be prepared ahead, so on Christmas Day she would be as free as a bird. "Will you at least put a beef tenderloin in the oven?" I asked. "Yes, I will do that, but little more," she said. I took up the challenge. This is the menu I designed, and it worked. Here are the blueprints.

# ROQUEFORT-STUFFED CELERY CURLS

This is an old favorite—and still one of the most attractive hors d'oeuvres there is.

*3 bunches white celery hearts or inner ribs of celery*
*¼ pound Roquefort cheese, at room temperature*
*½ cup (1 stick) unsalted butter, at room temperature*
*Salt to taste (optional)*

1. Cut the celery into 3-inch pieces. Using a sharp paring knife, make multiple ½-inch-long cuts at both ends, spacing the cuts close together so as to feather the ends. Drop the celery into a large bowl of ice water and leave in the refrigerator for several hours or as long as overnight. The feathered ends will curl up beautifully.
2. Combine the Roquefort cheese and butter in a small bowl and cream them together until the mixture is well blended and smooth. Taste and add salt if needed.
3. When you are ready to serve the celery, drain it well and pat the pieces dry. Fill the centers with the Roquefort mixture and arrange the celery on a serving platter.

Serves 8 or more

VARIATION:
Mix the Roquefort with cream cheese instead of butter.

You can prepare this hors d'oeuvre ahead. Cover the stuffed celery curls lightly with plastic wrap and store them in the refrigerator for up to 24 hours.

# MARINATED BEEF TENDERLOIN WITH OLD ENGLISH WALNUT SAUCE

This elegant dish is easy to prepare. Set the tenderloin in the marinade in the morning, roast it in the evening, and there you are! You can also make it ahead of time and serve it at room temperature—very thinly sliced, please.

## MARINADE
1 cup extra-virgin olive oil
½ cup dry red wine
1½ teaspoons dried tarragon
Salt to taste
1 teaspoon coarsely ground black pepper

## TENDERLOIN
1 beef tenderloin (4 to 5 pounds)
3 tablespoons extra-virgin olive oil
Salt
10 tablespoons (1¼ sticks) unsalted butter
Freshly ground black pepper to taste
Watercress sprigs, for garnish
Old English Walnut Sauce (optional; recipe follows)

1. Combine the marinade ingredients in a ceramic or stainless-steel bowl or baking dish. Blend well. Place the beef in the marinade and turn to coat it thoroughly. Leave the beef in the marinade, covered and refrigerated, for the day or up to 24 hours, turning it or brushing it with the marinade several times.
2. Preheat the oven to 500°F.
3. Lift the tenderloin from the marinade and drain it thoroughly. Brush the meat well with the olive oil and sprinkle it with salt.

4. Place the tenderloin in a roasting pan (on a rack if you like) and roast for 25 to 35 minutes, until an instant-reading thermometer reads 120°F to 125° F (for rare meat). Turn off the oven and let the meat rest inside for 5 to 10 minutes.

5. Remove the tenderloin from the pan and add 2 tablespoons butter to the pan. Heat the pan juices and butter, stirring, until the butter has melted. Keep warm.

6. In a separate pan, melt the remaining 8 tablespoons butter. Keep warm.

7. Carve the tenderloin into thin slices. Sprinkle the slices with salt and pepper and pour the melted butter over them. Pour the reserved pan juices over the slices as well. Garnish with watercress and serve the Old English Walnut Sauce alongside if you like (the butter sauce is quite delectable on its own).

Serves 8 to 10 (a ½-pound serving each)

Tenderloin should always be served rare, as it dries out when cooked longer. If any slices are too rare, cover them with a few spoonfuls of the pan juices and butter and place them in the oven for a few seconds (no longer).

Tenderloin is delicious served cold, sliced very thin, with Walnut Sauce, as a salad. It also makes delectable small, cold hors d'oeuvre sandwiches or heartier sandwiches for Sunday night suppers. Use your finest and freshest bread.

## OLD ENGLISH WALNUT SAUCE

This fine old walnut sauce, brought to us by the English in the eighteenth century, is wonderful with all kinds of simply prepared game, roasts (not stews, however), and especially fish. The meat or fish should be prepared rather plain to be a good background for the sauce.

The walnuts for this recipe are processed when they are green. They are taken from their outer coating, then dried and pickled. It is a tedious ordeal, and to my mind the English are still the only ones who do it well. They are expensive now and are to be found only at gourmet shops and grocery stores that deal in very special items. There are only a few companies that do the walnuts; the best are from George Watkins in London.

*1 cup juice from two 10-ounce jars of pickled walnuts,*
    *George Watkins brand if possible*
*4 pickled walnuts*
*2 teaspoons anchovy paste*
*2 teaspoons peeled and chopped shallots*
*1 teaspoon brandy or cognac*

Combine all the ingredients in a small saucepan and simmer over a low heat for 2 minutes. Spoon into a blender or food processor and purée. Store in a clean jar in the refrigerator (this sauce will keep indefinitely).

Makes 1 cup

Keep the remaining walnuts in the refrigerator to use with roasts and steaks. They will keep indefinitely with very little juice, but they must be kept cold.

## WILD RICE

Any rice, including wild rice, can be cooked ahead. Cover and refrigerate the cooked rice. At dinnertime, heat it quickly in a microwave or, tightly covered with foil, in a preheated 425°F oven.

*2 cups wild rice*
*6 cups water*
*½ cup (1 stick) unsalted butter, at room temperature*
*Salt to taste*

1.   Wash the rice thoroughly in a bowl of cold water, changing the water several times, and then drain.
2.   Bring the 6 cups water to a hard boil in a large saucepan. Add the rice and boil until it has puffed a bit and is tender but still a little chewy (*al dente*). This will take 20 to 25 minutes.
3.   Drain the rice at once, add the butter and salt, and toss with a fork.

Serves 6 to 8

# VELVET CRUMB ROLLS

This exquisite, velvety dough will be a great joy to you, as it has been to so many of my students and to me. You can do all kinds of things with it, as it is such a versatile formula.

*1 package dry yeast*
*¼ cup lukewarm water*
*1 large mealy potato, peeled and chopped*
*6 tablespoons unsalted butter, at room temperature*
*2 tablespoons sugar*
*2 large eggs*
*1 cup sour cream*
*2 teaspoons salt*
*5 cups sifted all-purpose flour*
*3 tablespoons unsalted butter, melted, for brushing the rolls*

1.   Dissolve the yeast in the lukewarm water. Set aside.
2.   Boil the potato, well covered with water, until soft. Drain the potato, but reserve the potato water and keep it warm.
3.   Sieve or rice the potato and measure 1 cup of it into a large bowl. *Do not put it in a food processor.*

4. Add the butter, sugar, and ¼ cup of the reserved warm potato water and mix well. When the butter has melted, add the eggs, sour cream, and dissolved yeast. Beat thoroughly by hand or with an electric mixer. Add the salt and flour, beating the mixture hard.

5. Toss the dough onto a lightly floured surface. Knead heavily, adding enough flour to make the dough smooth and elastic but not sticky. Place the dough in a lightly greased bowl and turn it to coat all sides. Cover the bowl with plastic wrap, place in a warm, draft-free spot, and allow the dough to rise until doubled in bulk, about 1 hour.

6. When the dough has risen, punch it down lightly. Cover the bowl again with plastic wrap and refrigerate until the dough is well chilled, about 2 hours, or as long as overnight.

7. When the dough has chilled, turn it out onto a lightly floured surface and divide it in half. Roll each half into a circle about ¼ inch thick. Cut into rounds with a biscuit cutter, roll the rounds into balls, and place in lightly greased muffin tins (each cup should be about ⅔ full). Cover the tins with plastic wrap, place in a warm, draft-free spot, and allow the rolls to rise until doubled in bulk and light and springy, about 1 hour.

8. While the dough is rising, preheat the oven to 400°F.

9. When the dough has risen, place the tins on the lower rack of the preheated oven and bake until the rolls are golden brown, about 15 to 20 minutes. Brush immediately with the melted butter and serve.

Makes 30 to 36 rolls

VARIATIONS:

*Glazed Rolls:* Before baking, the rolls may be brushed with a glaze made from 1 beaten egg yolk and 2 tablespoons heavy or whipping cream.

*Poppy Seed or Sesame Seed Rolls:* After glazing and before baking, sprinkle the rolls with poppy seeds or sesame seeds. If you use sesame seeds, you will have to toast them beforehand, as they will not toast sufficiently on the rolls to bring out their nutty flavor.

*Velvet Crumb Bread:* This recipe also makes wonderful bread. Before the second rise, place each half of the dough in a lightly greased standard-size loaf pan.

And for a sweeter bread, increase the amount of sugar in the recipe, up to 4 tablespoons.

> Day-old rolls may be split, buttered, sprinkled with poppy seeds, and toasted in a preheated 450°F oven. This makes for a crisper roll than one that is broiled under a flame, and it is a superb way to revitalize any roll that is not oven-fresh, or even a slice of bread that is not delightfully fresh.

### How to Make Different Roll Shapes

**Cloverleaf Rolls:** Before the second rise, roll small balls of dough in the palms of your hands. Put 3 balls, edges touching, in each cup of the greased muffin tins. Cover with plastic wrap and allow to rise until doubled in bulk. Bake in a preheated 375°F oven. Brush immediately with melted butter after baking.

**Bowknot Rolls:** Before the second rise, roll thin ropes of dough. Cut and tie in bowknots. Place on greased pastry sheets. Cover with plastic wrap and allow to rise until doubled in bulk. Bake in a preheated 375°F oven. Brush immediately with melted butter after baking.

**Braided Rolls:** Before the second rise, roll the dough into a long rectangle about ¼ inch thick. Cut lengthwise into 3 even strips. Braid as you would 3 ribbons. Cut in desired lengths for rolls. Place on greased pastry sheets. Cover with plastic wrap and allow to rise until doubled in bulk. Bake in a preheated 375°F oven. Brush immediately with melted butter after baking.

**Crescent or Horn Rolls:** Before the second rise, roll the dough into a circle, as if making a pie crust. Cut in even wedge-shaped pieces. Roll each piece from the outside in. Place an inch apart on greased pastry sheets. Cover with plastic wrap and allow to rise until doubled in bulk. Bake in a preheated 350°F oven. Brush immediately with melted butter after baking.

**Biscuits:** Before the second rise, roll out the dough to a thickness of about ¼ inch. Cut in rounds with a biscuit cutter. Place on greased pastry sheets. Cover with plastic wrap and allow to rise until doubled in bulk. Bake in a preheated 375°F oven. Brush immediately with melted butter after baking.

**Parker House Rolls:** Before the second rise, roll out the dough to a thickness of about ¼ inch. Cut in rounds with a biscuit cutter. Dip each round in melted butter, covering both sides well. Fold one side up to meet the center. Place on greased pastry sheets with the edges touching; if they do not touch, the rolls will spring open. Cover with plastic wrap and allow to rise until doubled in bulk. Bake in a preheated 375°F oven. Brush immediately with melted butter after baking.

## BIBB LETTUCE, ENDIVE, AND SPICED WALNUT SALAD

This is delectable as a separate course before or after the entrée. For an informal holiday meal, serve it with a good soup, homemade bread, and dessert.

### WALNUT OIL VINAIGRETTE
*6 tablespoons walnut oil*
*3 tablespoons vegetable oil*
*3 tablespoons champagne vinegar or other premium-quality*
*    white wine vinegar*
*Salt to taste*
*Fresh lemon juice (optional)*

### SALAD
*2 heads Bibb lettuce*
*2 heads Belgian endive*
*1 cup Spiced Walnuts (see page 91), prepared with walnut halves or*
*    large pieces (do not chop the nuts)*

1.  Combine the vinaigrette ingredients in a small bowl or jar and blend thoroughly, adding the lemon juice if it's needed. Set the dressing aside.
2.  Separate the lettuce and endive leaves, rinse them, and pat them dry. (You can refrigerate them for a few hours if you want to prepare the salad ahead.)
3.  When you are ready to serve the salad, arrange the Bibb lettuce leaves in a shallow serving bowl. Cut the endive leaves into slivers and scatter them over the lettuce. Spoon the Spiced Walnuts into a mound in the center.
4.  Take the salad bowl to the table, add the vinaigrette, and toss carefully (use just enough dressing to coat the greens lightly).

Serves 4

## TANGERINE SHERBET

The flavor of tangerines is very special and unique, even though it is so closely related to that of the orange. Tangerine sherbet makes a perfect dessert for Christmas holiday meals. Tangerines are at the peak of their season then, and this recipe makes a stunning dessert when served in icy cold sherbet glasses garnished with a few thin, ice-cold tangerine slices or with one or two tiny whole kumquats with their leaves still attached.

*3 cups water*
*2 cups sugar*
*4 cups fresh tangerine juice, chilled*
*Juice of 1 lemon, or to taste*
*1 egg white (optional)*

1.  Combine the water and sugar in a large saucepan and boil until the sugar has dissolved and the syrup is clear, about 2 minutes. Set the syrup in the refrigerator to chill.

2.  Combine the chilled syrup and the tangerine juice. Blend well and add the lemon juice. Pour the mixture into a stainless-steel bowl and freeze it for 10 hours or overnight.
3.  Whip the frozen mixture thoroughly with an electric hand mixer. In a small bowl, beat the egg white with a few tablespoons of the sherbet until the mixture is foamy. Spoon the egg white into the sherbet and whip it thoroughly again.
4.  Return the sherbet to the freezer and let it freeze rather hard, 3 to 4 hours (or overnight). One or 2 hours before serving, whip the sherbet again.

Serves 6 to 8

You can make this sherbet in an electric ice-cream freezer—simply freeze the sherbet according to the manufacturer's directions. Just before it has finished freezing, beat the egg white with a little of the sherbet and add it to the sherbet.

This is a fragile sherbet and best if eaten within 24 hours. If you want to keep it for longer than 2 or 3 days, omit the egg white.

## WINTER CRYSTAL COOKIES

This has been a favorite butter cookie among my students. It is perfect to accompany sherbet or ice cream.

1 cup (2 sticks) unsalted butter, at room temperature
1 cup sugar
3 large egg yolks
2½ cups sifted all-purpose flour
2¼ teaspoons baking powder

*½ teaspoon salt*
*2 teaspoons pure vanilla extract or cognac vanilla (see page 29),*
   *or 1 tablespoon cognac or Grand Marnier*
*¾ cup sugar crystals or turbinado sugar*

1. Cream the butter and sugar together with an electric mixer or in a food processor.
2. Add the egg yolks and mix thoroughly.
3. Add the flour, baking powder, salt, and vanilla. Blend well. Cover the dough with plastic wrap and refrigerate until it is firm enough to be rolled into balls, about 1 hour.
4. Preheat the oven to 350°F.
5. Pick off tablespoon-size chunks of dough and roll them into ball shapes. Place them on a very lightly greased pastry sheet and sprinkle them with a little of the sugar. Flatten each ball to ⅛-inch thickness with your fingers or the bottom of a small glass that has been dipped in the sugar (the thinner the cookie, the crisper it will be).
6. Bake the cookies until they are just slightly browned, about 15 minutes. Watch them closely. If they've browned but don't seem done, turn off the oven, leave the door ajar, and let the cookies stay in the oven for another 10 to 15 minutes.
7. Remove the cookies from the pastry sheet and place them on wire racks to cool. Store them in an airtight tin or freeze them.

Makes about 36 cookies

You can prepare the dough and refrigerate it for a week or so before baking the cookies.

# A FIRESIDE
# HOLIDAY PICNIC

## MENU 13

*Smoked Breast of Chicken with Prunes*
*Ham in Rosemary Buns*
*Egg Salad Sandwiches with Capers and Tarragon*
*Classic English Fruitcake*
*Kentucky Bourbon Fruitcake Cookies*
*A Favorite Deep-South Pecan Cookie*
*Fabulous Chocolate Marionettes*
*Luscious Apricot-Orange Candy*
*St. Augustine Mincemeat Cookies*
*New Orleans Eggnog*
*Biscuit Tortoni*
*Coffee*

There are many different kinds and styles of food, and dozens of ways to celebrate Christmas, but a gathering of close friends and family around the warmth and glow of a fireside, with baskets of yummy sandwiches from the bountiful leftovers, is rather special. I love it, and I believe you will too.

## SMOKED BREAST OF CHICKEN WITH PRUNES

A very special Christmas tea sandwich—it's also perfect for a fireside Christmas picnic.

*½ cup dried pitted prunes*
*⅓ cup Cointreau, Spanish sherry, or Grand Marnier*
*¼ pound smoked chicken or pheasant breast*
*2½ tablespoons unsalted butter, at room temperature*
*1 loaf whole-wheat bread, thinly sliced*
*Large fresh walnut halves, for serving*

1. Several days before the picnic, combine the prunes and the Cointreau in a small bowl. Cover and set aside to marinate at room temperature for at least 1 day, or better, for 2 to 3 days.
2. On the day of the picnic, drain the marinated prunes and cut them into thin slivers.
3. Slice the chicken or pheasant breast paper-thin. Spread butter over half of the bread slices and arrange the chicken on top. Scatter the prunes over the chicken. Spread butter over the remaining bread slices and place them over the filling, pressing slightly to seal the sandwiches.
4. Trim the crusts from the bread and cut the sandwiches into triangles or rectangles. Serve on a platter, accompanied by a bowl of walnuts.

Makes 10 to 15 sandwiches

Now stir the fire, and close
   the shutters fast,
Let fall the curtains, wheel
   the sofa round,
And, while the bubbling
   and loud-hissing urn
Throws up a steamy
   column, and the cups,
That cheer but not
   inebriate, wait on each,
So let us welcome peaceful
   evening in.

—William Cowper

## HAM IN ROSEMARY BUNS

These rosemary buns were created especially for these ham sandwiches, which have long been a specialty of mine for fireside Christmas picnics. They are assembled the day before and each one is wrapped in foil. A tiny hole is punched in the foil so that when they are heated just before serving they will not become sodden from the steam. How many you make depends largely upon the number you have invited to the party, but make plenty. Everyone loves them!

### ROSEMARY BUNS
1 package dry yeast
1 cup warm water
3 to 3½ cups sifted all-purpose flour
1 tablespoon sugar
1½ teaspoons salt
2 tablespoons solid vegetable shortening
1 large egg, separated
½ teaspoon fresh rosemary, or ¾ teaspoon dried rosemary, crumbled
2 tablespoons white cornmeal
1½ teaspoons cold water
Boiling water

### SANDWICH FILLING
1 cup sour cream
1 cup mayonnaise
1½ tablespoons Dijon mustard, or to taste
1 pound best-quality baked ham, thinly sliced

1.  Combine the yeast and ¼ cup of the warm water in a small bowl and stir to dissolve the yeast. Set it aside.

2. Sift 3 cups of the flour, the sugar, and the salt together into a large bowl. Using a pastry blender, cut in the shortening until the mixture resembles coarse cornmeal.

3. Add the dissolved yeast, the egg white, and the remaining ¾ cup warm water to the flour mixture. Stir thoroughly.

4. Transfer the dough to a lightly floured surface. Sprinkle the rosemary over the dough and knead the dough thoroughly, using the heel of your hand. If the dough is sticky, add a little more flour. It should feel soft and malleable, but it shouldn't stick to your fingers.

5. Place the dough in a greased bowl and turn it to grease all sides. Cover the bowl with plastic wrap and leave it in a warm place until the dough has doubled in bulk, about 1 hour.

6. Punch down the dough, place it on a lightly floured surface, and knead it lightly to remove any air bubbles.

7. Divide the dough in half. Using a dough scraper, cut each half into 6 pieces. (If you want to be sure they're truly even in size, weigh them; each should weigh about 2 ounces.) Roll each piece into a ball and turn the edges under so the top and sides of the bun are smooth.

8. Spread the cornmeal on a pastry sheet and dip the bottom of each bun in the cornmeal (this keeps the buns from sticking). Arrange the buns on a nonstick pastry sheet and cover them lightly with plastic wrap. Leave the buns in a warm spot until they have doubled in bulk, 30 to 40 minutes.

9. Meanwhile, preheat the oven to 400°F.

10. Whisk the egg yolk and the cold water together thoroughly. Using a small brush, paint each bun with this egg wash.

11. Pour boiling water into a shallow baking pan and place it on the bottom of the oven. (The steam from the water will make a nice crisp crust.) Place the pastry sheet on the middle rack and bake the buns until the tops are a deep golden brown, 20 to 25 minutes. Allow the buns to cool before making the sandwiches.

12. For the sandwiches, preheat the oven to 350°F.

13. In a mixing bowl, combine the sour cream, mayonnaise, and mustard. Stir together thoroughly.

14. Cut open the buns and spread the sauce lavishly on both halves. Arrange the ham on the bottom halves and close the buns.

15. Wrap each sandwich in aluminum foil and punch a small hole in the side (this hole acts as an air vent and keeps the sandwich from becoming sodden).

16. Place the wrapped sandwiches on a baking sheet and heat them on the middle rack of the preheated oven for about 15 minutes (the cooking time varies with sandwich size).

17. Don't unwrap the sandwiches when they come out of the oven. Arrange them in a charming basket and pass them to the guests sitting around the cozy fireside having fun.

Makes 12 sandwiches

VARIATION:
Combine sliced turkey or chicken breast with the ham, or make the sandwiches all of chicken breast.

If you're expecting a large crowd, double the recipe—but use only 1½ packages of yeast.

Rosemary and sage are the only herbs that are stronger when fresh than when they are dried.

The dough for the Rosemary Buns is not unlike a French bread dough, but using water instead of milk and shortening instead of butter.

The buns freeze well; just thaw them and reheat them in a 400°F oven. No wonder they won a blue ribbon at the state fair.


## EGG SALAD SANDWICHES WITH CAPERS AND TARRAGON

We must never take eggs for granted. They are one of our greatest treasures, and our kitchens and tables would be sad affairs without them. The egg salad tea sandwiches given here are a case in point. Capers are a luxury now, but they are soul mates to eggs (as well as to fish and chicken salad).

A few days ahead, replace the vinegar in a bottle of capers with white wine tarragon vinegar. (Capers were always pickled in tarragon vinegar in times gone by. Then the tarragon was omitted because of the expense.) Capers marinated in tarragon vinegar are almost a prerequisite for a flavorful egg or chicken salad.

*6 hard-cooked eggs, finely chopped*
*3 tablespoons mayonnaise, or more if needed*
*1 teaspoon Dijon mustard*
*1½ teaspoons capers*
*1 teaspoon white wine tarragon vinegar*
*Salt and freshly ground white pepper to taste*
*Dash of cayenne pepper*
*12 thin slices white bread*
*Watercress sprigs, for garnish*

1. In a mixing bowl, combine the eggs, mayonnaise, and mustard. Stir to combine. Add the capers, vinegar, salt, white pepper, and cayenne. Mix well. Taste and adjust the seasonings if necessary. If the mixture seems too dry, add another tablespoon of mayonnaise.
2. Spread the filling on 6 slices of bread and top with the remaining slices, pressing them down slightly. Trim off the crusts and cut the sandwiches into small triangles. Keep well covered with plastic wrap or aluminum foil and refrigerate until serving time.
3. Arrange the sandwiches on a platter, garnish with watercress, and serve.

Makes 18 small sandwiches

Don't make these sandwiches more than 2 hours ahead. The filling is moist and they'll turn sodden if held too long.

## CLASSIC ENGLISH FRUITCAKE

Down through the ages, bread was considered man's most valuable food, but cake or sweetened breads long ago became a symbol of celebrations such as the Yuletide feasts. And there is nothing—with the exception of the decorated and highly lit evergreen tree—that speaks more strongly of Christmas than fruitcake.

We inherited the making of fruitcakes, puddings, and mincemeats from our English ancestors. The formulas for these holiday sweets have remained a classic culinary art that we have never betrayed. We revere them as they have come down to us through the ages.

A fine fruitcake is testimony of a superb baker and cook, and one who loves the art. The selection of the best ingredients comes first, then the wisdom of the baker.

When properly cared for, fruitcakes mellow with time, and they are, without a doubt, one of the great joys of the holiday table.

In England and on the Continent, brandy was usually used in fruitcakes. In the Deep South, rum was popular, but in Virginia and Kentucky, bourbon was used. The choice is up to you. I prefer cognac, but a fine bourbon tastes not unlike a good brandy.

½ cup cognac, Jamaica rum, or good-quality bourbon
1 cup pitted dates, sliced
1½ cups dark Mission figs, chopped
½ cup dried pitted prunes, chopped
1 cup dark sticky raisins, chopped (see owl, page 144)
2½ cups mixed glacéed fruits, including apricots, pineapple, citron,
　　　angelica, currants, orange peel, and lemon peel
2¼ cups sifted all-purpose flour
1 teaspoon salt
¼ teaspoon baking soda

1 teaspoon baking powder
2 teaspoons ground cinnamon
1 teaspoon ground allspice
1 teaspoon ground cloves
½ teaspoon ground coriander
¾ cup (1½ sticks) unsalted butter, at room temperature
1½ cups dark brown sugar
4 large eggs
½ cup heavy or whipping cream
⅓ to ½ cup cognac, Jamaica rum, or good-quality bourbon, for
    basting the cakes in storage

1. Combine the ½ cup cognac and all the fruits in a large bowl. Stir and allow
   to marinate overnight, covered.
2. Preheat the oven to 250°F. Lightly grease 2 loaf pans and line them with
   aluminum foil. Set them aside.
3. Sift the flour, salt, baking soda, baking powder, and spices together into a
   large bowl.
4. Using an electric mixer, cream the butter and brown sugar together in a
   large bowl. Add the eggs and mix thoroughly.
5. Alternating, gradually add the cream and the flour mixture, beating thoroughly. Do not overbeat.
6. Stir in the marinated fruits by hand. Divide the batter between the prepared pans, leaving a ¾-inch space at the top.
7. Bake on the middle rack of the preheated oven until a knife inserted in the
   center comes out clean, from 2 to 2½ hours (test after 2 hours). Let the
   cakes cool in the pans. Then turn them out onto a rack and baste with
   some of the cognac. Wrap each cake in a clean cloth, place them in an airtight tin or plastic container, and store in a cool place or in the refrigerator
   for at least 2 weeks. Check the cakes once a week and if the cloths have
   dried out, baste the cakes again with cognac. The cakes will keep for
   months this way.

Makes 2 loaf cakes

Black sticky raisins, which I prefer, are seeded before they are dried. The raisins that rattle in the box are made of Thompson seedless grapes, and I don't recommend them. I like Sunsweet brand raisins.

You can bake this cake in a tube pan or mold if you like. The larger pan may require a longer baking time, so watch it carefully.

## KENTUCKY BOURBON FRUITCAKE COOKIES

This treasured Christmas cookie freezes beautifully. I use only Australian glazed fruits; Italian glazed citron is excellent also (you can find it in gourmet shops).

½ cup sugar
Zest of ½ navel orange
Zest of ½ lemon
4 tablespoons (½ stick) unsalted butter, at room temperature
2 large eggs, lightly beaten
1½ cups sifted all-purpose flour
1½ teaspoons baking powder
¼ teaspoon salt
1 teaspoon ground cinnamon
½ teaspoon ground allspice
¼ teaspoon ground cloves
⅓ cup bourbon
½ pound seedless raisins, chopped
¼ pound dried currants
¼ pound glazed citron, finely chopped
½ pound dried pitted prunes or dark Mission figs, coarsely slivered
¼ to ½ pound glazed or dried apricots, slivered
3 cups coarsely chopped pecans
Bourbon or Bourbon Glaze (recipe follows), for topping (optional)

1. Preheat the oven to 250°F. Lightly grease 2 cookie sheets (or use nonstick cookie sheets).
2. Combine the sugar, orange zest, and lemon zest in a food processor and twirl until the zest is finely grated (or grate the zest by hand and add it to the sugar).
3. Combine the sugar mixture and butter in a food processor or with an electric mixer and blend until creamy. Add the eggs and mix well.
4. Sift together the flour, baking powder, salt, and spices. Add them to the egg mixture. Add the bourbon and mix thoroughly.
5. Stir all the fruits and the nuts into the batter by hand.
6. Drop the batter by teaspoonfuls onto the prepared cookie sheets and bake on the middle rack of the preheated oven until the cookies feel rather firm, about 20 to 25 minutes. Brush the warm cookies with bourbon or the Bourbon Glaze, or leave them plain. Let them cool on wire racks and then store in an airtight tin.

Makes about 75 cookies

VARIATION:
*Tiny Fruitcakes:* Butter 1- or 1½-inch tart pans and fill them with the batter. Bake for about 25 minutes (the time for baking the tiny fruitcakes varies with the size of the little pans that are used). Glaze or leave plain.

Plump, moist pitted prunes in sealed tins are available in most supermarkets —an excellent product.

## BOURBON GLAZE

*1½ cups sifted confectioners' sugar*
*2 tablespoons bourbon plus 2 tablespoons water, or 4 tablespoons bourbon*

Place the sifted confectioners' sugar in a mixing bowl and blend in the bourbon and water until smooth.

Makes 1½ cups

# A Favorite Deep-South Pecan Cookie

This is a very old-fashioned cookie that's almost unique to the South, where pecan trees grow. I have seen it translated using almonds, but that misses the mark of distinction the pecan flavor lends to the cookie. It keeps for weeks in a tin box in the refrigerator, or for months when frozen.

¾ cup (1½ sticks) unsalted butter, at room temperature
½ teaspoon salt
6 tablespoons confectioners' sugar
2 cups sifted all-purpose flour
1 tablespoon water
1½ teaspoons pure vanilla extract or cognac vanilla (see page 29)
2 cups pecans, chopped very fine (but not ground)
¾ cup confectioners' sugar, for rolling

1. Combine the butter, salt, and 6 tablespoons confectioners' sugar in a food processor or with an electric mixer and blend. Add the flour, water, and vanilla and blend until you have a soft dough.
2. Stir the pecans into the dough by hand.
3. Cover the dough with aluminum foil and refrigerate it—overnight if possible—for the pecan flavor to permeate.
4. Preheat the oven to 300°F. Very lightly grease 2 cookie sheets or (better) use nonstick cookie sheets.
5. Work the chilled dough well with your hands to make it malleable and then roll it into small "fingers," about 2 inches long and 1½ inches wide. Place the cookies 1½ inches apart on the prepared cookie sheets and bake until the bottoms of the cookies are a very light brown, about 30 minutes (the rest of the cookie remains almost white).
6. Remove the cookies from the oven and let them cool slightly. Then roll them in the confectioners' sugar and allow to cool thoroughly.

Makes 48 cookies

## Fabulous Chocolate Marionettes

I call these special cookies "marionettes" because marionettes are among the most charming of all the small French sweets. They are tiny bite-size things, half cake and half tart, made in minuscule French tins. They keep exceedingly well and will freeze. Marionettes are wonderful to serve when a "pickup" bite of sweetness is called for, or for holiday receptions, buffet suppers, and fireside picnics.

If the tiny pans are unavailable, these marionettes may be baked as you would any cookie, but don't expect them to be as intriguing.

### MARIONETTES
½ cup (1 stick) unsalted butter, at room temperature
1 cup firmly packed light brown sugar
2 large eggs, lightly beaten
2 ounces semisweet chocolate, melted
1 teaspoon pure vanilla extract, or 1 tablespoon cognac
1½ cups sifted all-purpose flour
¼ teaspoon salt
¼ teaspoon baking soda
1 teaspoon baking powder
½ cup buttermilk or sour cream
1 cup chopped walnuts, pecans, hazelnuts, or unblanched almonds

### FROSTING
1½ cups sifted confectioners' sugar
4½ teaspoons unsweetened cocoa powder
2 tablespoons unsalted butter, melted
1 teaspoon pure vanilla extract or cognac vanilla (see page 29)
3 to 4 tablespoons heavy or whipping cream

1. Preheat the oven to 325°F. Grease 24 to 36 tiny tart tins (2 or 2¾-inch × ½-inch tins, not fluted).

2.  Combine the butter and brown sugar with an electric mixer and cream until smooth. Add the eggs and beat hard until the batter is thick and smooth. Add the melted chocolate and the vanilla.
3.  Sift the flour together with the salt, baking soda, and baking powder. Alternating, gradually add the flour and the buttermilk to the chocolate mixture, stirring thoroughly. Mix in the nuts by hand.
4.  Spoon the batter into the prepared tart tins, filling them not quite all the way. Bake on the middle rack of the preheated oven until the marionettes spring back at once when touched with your finger, 10 to 15 minutes.
5.  While the marionettes are baking, blend the frosting ingredients together, using enough cream to make the frosting smooth.
6.  Remove the marionettes from the oven and immediately spread the frosting quite thickly over them. When the marionettes are cool, run a thin sharp knife around the edges and release them from the tins.

Makes 24 to 36 marionettes

VARIATION:
*Chocolate Marron Marionettes:* Cover 1 cup drained, coarsely chopped marrons (preserved chestnuts in syrup) with brandy and store in an airtight jar for several days or as long as a week (the longer the better). Use the marrons in place of the nuts. Season the frosting with 1½ tablespoons brandy or cognac, in addition to the vanilla, and garnish each frosted marionette with a thick slice of marron.

Depending on the size of your tart tins, you may need to double the amount of frosting.

## LUSCIOUS APRICOT-ORANGE CANDY

This recipe, given to me by a French student, couldn't be easier or more delicious. You can make the candy weeks before

Christmas and hide it in your refrigerator—but hide it well. Otherwise, when Christmas comes, you may find the candy has disappeared!

*1 navel orange*
*1 pound dried apricots, cut into small pieces*
*2 cups superfine sugar*
*½ cup sugar crystals*

1.  Cut the orange in half and remove any seeds. Cut the halves into smaller pieces and place them in a food processor along with the apricots. Process until finely mashed.
2.  Transfer the orange-apricot mixture to the top of a double boiler and add the superfine sugar. Cook over simmering water until the sugar has completely dissolved and the mixture is not grainy, 5 to 6 minutes.
3.  Place the mixture in the refrigerator until thoroughly chilled, about 35 to 40 minutes.
4.  Form small balls of the orange-apricot mixture by rolling pieces between the palms of your hands. Place the sugar crystals in a shallow bowl and toss the candy balls in the sugar to coat them well. Refrigerate until ready to serve.

Makes 1 pound

VARIATIONS:
*With nuts:* After the mixture has cooked in the double boiler, stir in ¼ to ½ cup chopped blanched almonds. Or you can roll the candy in finely chopped blanched almonds instead of the sugar crystals.

*With Grand Marnier:* Add 1 tablespoon Grand Marnier to the orange-apricot mixture before chilling.

# St. Augustine Mincemeat Cookies

St. Augustine Mincemeat is too sweet and rich for a 9-inch pie, but it is lovely for small turnovers, very tiny tarts, and cookies.

½ cup (1 stick) unsalted butter, at room temperature
1 cup sugar
2 large eggs
2½ cups sifted all-purpose flour
2 teaspoons baking powder
½ teaspoon salt
1¼ cups St. Augustine Mincemeat (see page 229)
2 tablespoons chopped preserved ginger
1 cup coarsely chopped walnuts
1 teaspoon pure vanilla extract, or 1 to 1½ tablespoons cognac or brandy
Confectioners' sugar, for dusting

1. Preheat the oven to 350°F. Grease 2 cookie sheets (or use nonstick cookie sheets).
2. Cream the butter and sugar together with an electric mixer or in a food processor. Add the eggs and beat hard.
3. Sift the flour with the baking powder and salt and beat them into the egg mixture.
4. Fold in the mincemeat, ginger, nuts, and vanilla by hand.
5. Drop the batter by small spoonfuls onto the prepared cookie sheets, and bake on the middle rack of the preheated oven until the cookies are light brown, 15 to 20 minutes.
6. Cool the cookies on a rack and store them in an airtight container with wax paper between the layers. Before serving, dust them with confectioners' sugar.

Makes 30 cookies

## NEW ORLEANS EGGNOG

Louisiana has always had a great affection for rum, and rum makes a beloved Christmas punch for old New Orleans festivals and celebrations. This eggnog serves about twenty guests, but the recipe can be cut in half or even quartered. Just don't make it too far ahead.

*12 large eggs, separated*
*1 cup sugar*
*½ cup Jamaica rum*
*2½ cups best-quality bourbon*
*3 cups heavy or whipping cream*
*1 cup milk*
*1 to 1¼ cups heavy or whipping cream, whipped*
*Freshly grated nutmeg, for serving*

1. Combine the egg yolks with ½ cup of the sugar in a mixing bowl and beat until the mixture is creamy and thick. Add the rum and bourbon and beat thoroughly. Add the cream and milk and mix again.
2. Beat the egg whites until they hold a soft peak. Gradually add the remaining ½ cup sugar, beating until the whites hold a stiff peak. Fold them into the yolk mixture. Chill thoroughly until serving time.
3. Pour the eggnog into a chilled punch bowl and gently fold in the whipped cream. Grate nutmeg over the top and serve.

Makes about 30 small cups

If you make the eggnog ahead, it will liquify—and that's a very poor eggnog. Southern eggnog is rich and thick, so serve it soon after it is mixed.

## BISCUIT TORTONI

There are small crinkled aluminum foil muffin cups on the market today that are perfect for serving this frozen dessert to a crowd. It was named for Tortoni, one of the creators of ice cream in Italy. Biscuit Tortoni was originally made with crushed macaroons instead of almonds. It can still be made that way if you prefer, as it is quite pleasant indeed.

This dessert has always been a favorite in the South.

*¾ cup sugar*
*⅓ cup water*
*5 large egg yolks*
*2 cups heavy or whipping cream*
*3 tablespoons brandy, amaretto, or cognac*
*½ cup coarsely chopped toasted almonds*

1.  Combine the sugar and water in a small saucepan and boil until the sugar has dissolved and the mixture is clear, about 2 minutes.
2.  Beat the egg yolks with an electric mixer until they turn a shade lighter and fall in ribbons from a spoon, about 2 minutes. Pour the hot sugar syrup into the egg yolks in a steady stream, beating constantly. Continue to beat until the mixture is cool.

3. Whip the cream and fold it into the egg mixture. Add the brandy and ¼ cup of the almonds; blend thoroughly. Spoon the mixture into small dessert bowls or cups and sprinkle with the remaining ¼ cup almonds. Place in the freezer for 3 or 4 hours, or as long as overnight.
4. Remove the tortoni from the freezer 15 to 20 minutes before you plan to serve it so it will soften up a bit.

Serves 10 to 12

VARIATION:
Crumble 4 or 5 macaroons and add them to the mixture instead of the first ¼ cup almonds; however, use the other ¼ cup almonds, not macaroons, to garnish the tops.

# A CHRISTMAS TEA PARTY

*Tea Party Sandwiches: Sandwich Rolls,*
*Ribbon Sandwiches,*
*Pinwheel Sandwiches, and Sandwich Loaves*

*Hazelnut Marionettes, Almond Contessas,*
*Marvelous Gingersnaps, Mincemeat Turnovers,*
*Kathy's Dried Cherry Scones, and Ginger Roll with Marrons*

*The Chartwell Cake*

Tea

As Henry James so wisely said, "There are few hours in life more agreeable than the hour dedicated to the ceremony known as afternoon tea."

There are few things, indeed, more quieting and restful than a cup of tea in midafternoon on a very hectic day. It lifts our spirits and lets us pause in all the rush and hurry. It is to Anna, Duchess of Bedford, that we owe these blessings.

The story goes that Duchess Anna (1753–1857) grew faint during the long wait between lunch and the late hour of the royal dinner, so she requested her servant to bring her a cup of tea at four o'clock, and a bit of bread and butter and a sweet to tide her over. The news echoed throughout the palace with great speed and her ladies-in-waiting followed suit. The afternoon tea was born.

Whether it is just a cup of tea with a friend or a Christmas tea party, the menu should be elegant in its simplicity. The sandwiches should be fresh and flavorful, but they need not be elaborate. If by chance you have a small cake or cookie of which you are justly proud, that will add to the warmth and fun of the party. These are the things of which pleasant memories are made.

## Tea Party Sandwiches

Finger sandwiches are always lovely, but there are a number of ways to make tea sandwiches especially festive for your holiday gathering.

**Sandwich Rolls:** Chill a loaf of unsliced bread. Trim the crusts from the loaf and cut the bread into very thin slices. Spread each slice with filling and roll it up tightly. Line a baking pan with wax paper and lay the sandwiches in it, seam side down. Cover with a layer of aluminum foil, then a damp cloth. Refrigerate until ready to serve.

**Ribbon Sandwiches:** Chill one white and one whole-wheat loaf of unsliced bread. Trim off the crusts and cut the bread into ¼-inch-thick slices. Spread the filling over 3 slices and stack 4 slices together, alternating white and whole-wheat. Press firmly to compress the layers. Repeat with the remaining bread and filling. Wrap in foil and chill for several hours. When you're ready to serve the sandwiches, cut them into thin slices.

**Pinwheel Sandwiches:** Chill a loaf of unsliced bread. Trim the crusts from the loaf and cut the bread lengthwise into thin slices. Spread the slices with filling and roll them up tightly. Cover the rolls with foil and then with a damp cloth. Refrigerate for several hours. When you are ready to serve them, cut the rolls into thin slices.

**Sandwich Loaves:** Chill a loaf of unsliced bread. Trim off the crusts and cut the loaf lengthwise into ⅜-inch-thick slices. Spread the slices with fillings that are compatible in flavor and color and reform the loaf, topping it with a plain slice. Press the layers together well. Using an electric mixer, blend 1 pound cream cheese with ¼ cup heavy or whipping cream until perfectly smooth. Spread this mixture over the entire sandwich loaf. Cover and refrigerate. When ready to serve, slice and place on dainty plates garnished with watercress. (These sandwiches require a fork.)

Sandwiches are always best when made with really fresh bread. To slice the bread, chill it until it's almost frozen; then use a very sharp knife to cut it into thin slices.

To store tea sandwiches, arrange them in shallow baking pans and cover them well with foil (tuck it right under the sandwiches). Lay a damp towel on top of the foil and refrigerate. If the towel dries out, redampen it.

## SANDWICH FILLINGS

**Ham Pâté:** Grind up some lean ham—Smithfield, country ham, or prosciutto. Stir in a little soft unsalted butter, Dijon mustard to taste, and enough heavy cream to make a paste. Spread mayonnaise over the bread, then the ham pâté.

**Watercress:** Combine chopped watercress, finely chopped walnuts, and enough mayonnaise to hold the mixture together. Spread unsalted butter over the bread, then the watercress mixture. This is particularly attractive as a Pinwheel Sandwich.

**Chicken and Tongue:** Spread unsalted butter over thin slices of bread. Arrange thin slices of smoked chicken breast and smoked boiled tongue over the bread and sprinkle with finely chopped unsalted pistachio nuts. Roll the bread up tightly, secure with toothpicks, wrap in foil, and refrigerate. (This filling can also be used for flat finger sandwiches.)

**Cucumber:** In a mixing bowl, combine 1 or 2 sliced peeled cucumbers, ½ cup cider vinegar, ⅓ cup water, 3 tablespoons sugar, and salt to taste. Leave for 1 hour. Then drain the cucumbers thoroughly. Spread mayonnaise on thin rounds of fresh white bread, cover with the cucumber slices, and sprinkle with chopped fresh parsley or dill. Serve as open-face sandwiches.

**Roquefort and Avocado:** Mix ¼ cup Roquefort cheese with 1 cup puréed avocado. Season quickly with 1 tablespoon fresh lemon juice (this keeps the avocado from darkening). Salt if needed and spread on bread to make flat finger sandwiches or Sandwich Rolls.

**Roquefort and Olive:** Bring ½ pound Roquefort cheese, ½ pound cream cheese, and ½ cup (1 stick) unsalted butter to room temperature. Cream the cheeses and butter together until perfectly smooth. Blend in ½ cup chopped Niçoise olives and ½ cup chopped fresh parsley. This filling works well as a Pinwheel Sandwich.

**Pimento Cheese:** Grate 1 pound sharp natural cheddar cheese. Allow it to come to room temperature. In a food processor, combine the cheese with ½ cup mayonnaise until smooth. Add 1 small jar pimentos, drained and cut into small pieces. Mix well and add salt if needed.

**Benedictine:** With an electric mixer or in a food processor, combine ½ pound cream cheese, 1 grated seeded cucumber, 1 teaspoon onion juice, and finely chopped green bell pepper and salt to taste.

**Chicken Salad:** In a mixing bowl, combine 2 cups chopped cooked chicken, ¾ cup finely chopped celery, 1 cup mayonnaise, 3 tablespoons drained capers, and salt and cayenne pepper to taste. Mix well. This filling will keep for several days in the refrigerator.

**Mushroom:** Sauté finely chopped fresh mushrooms in butter. Bind with a small amount of rich béchamel sauce, just enough to hold the mushrooms together. Spread on thin slices of white bread, roll up the slices, and brush them all over with melted butter. Just before serving, toast in a preheated 425°F oven until a delicate brown.

**Asparagus:** Spread mayonnaise over thin slices of white bread. Lay one spear of well-drained cooked asparagus at one end of the slice and roll it up in the bread. Chill as described for Sandwich Rolls.

**Toasted Cheese:** Grate cold sharp natural cheddar cheese. Bring it to room temperature. With an electric mixer, in a food processor, or by hand, combine the cheese with a little mayonnaise or heavy cream and blend until smooth. Spread the cheese on thin slices of white bread and roll them up. Brush them all over with melted butter. Cover and refrigerate. Just before serving, toast in a preheated 425°F oven until delicately browned. These sandwiches can be frozen, then thawed and toasted—but they can't be toasted ahead of time. (You can also make them with a mixture of Roquefort, cream cheese, and cream.)

**Crabmeat and Capers:** Flake 1 cup crabmeat and mix it with 3 tablespoons mayonnaise and 1½ tablespoons drained capers. Season to taste with lemon juice, salt, and cayenne pepper.

**Crabmeat and Egg:** Mix 2 cups flaked crabmeat with ½ cup finely chopped celery and 1 chopped hard-cooked egg. Add enough mayonnaise to bind the mixture and season to taste with lemon juice, salt, and cayenne pepper.

**Chicken and Almond Pâté:** Combine 2 cups ground white chicken meat with ½ cup chopped slivered almonds. Add enough mayonnaise to bind the mixture. Cut out rounds of white bread and spread them with the filling. Spread a bit of mayonnaise on the edge of the sandwiches and dip in chopped fresh parsley.

**Smoked Salmon:** Generously butter thin slices of pumpernickel bread and arrange tissue-paper-thin slices of smoked salmon over them. Cover with a second piece of buttered bread and cut into small triangles or rectangles. (You can also serve these as open-face sandwiches.)

**Chopped Cornish Hen:** Chop freshly poached Cornish hens (or chicken breasts) evenly but not too fine. If you like, stir in a few chopped walnuts. Add enough mayonnaise to bind the mixture and spread on unbuttered slices of pumpernickel bread. Top with another slice of bread and cut into generous "fingers."

## HAZELNUT MARIONETTES

These marionettes and the variations given here evolved out of my many years of baking and my fondness for hazelnuts. The crust is tender and crisp, and they keep well in a tight tin or may be frozen. They look very French—which they are, of course—and are exquisite indeed when served on a silver platter, to be eaten as a last delectable bite of sweet with coffee. They can be baked in small tart tins or formed into small cookies.

*½ cup (1 stick) unsalted butter, at room temperature*
*¼ cup sugar*
*¼ cup ground hazelnuts*
*1 cup sifted all-purpose flour*
*1 teaspoon pure vanilla extract or cognac vanilla (see page 29)*
*Red raspberry preserves (with seeds)*
*Coarsely chopped hazelnuts, for topping*
*Confectioners' sugar, for dusting*

1. Preheat the oven to 325°F. Grease 25 to 30 tiny tart tins (1¼ or 2 inches across, ½ inch deep—the smaller the better).

2. Combine the butter and sugar in a mixing bowl and cream together thoroughly. Add the ground hazelnuts, flour, and vanilla and blend well. Cream the dough with your hands until it is well mixed and smooth (mixing with your hands keeps the dough lighter).
3. Using your fingers, press the dough into the prepared tart tins. Make a shallow indentation in the center of each one. Place the tart tins on pastry sheets and bake on the middle rack of the preheated oven until the marionettes are light golden brown, 10 to 15 minutes.
4. Remove the marionettes from their tins and fill the center of each one with a teaspoon of raspberry preserves. Sprinkle the chopped nuts over the preserves. Allow the marionettes to cool. Just before serving, sift confectioners' sugar over the tops.

Makes 25 to 30 marionettes

VARIATIONS:
*Hazelnut and Chocolate Marionettes:* Instead of the preserves, fill the marionettes with melted sweet dark chocolate or semisweet chocolate. Decorate the top with a whole hazelnut and omit the confectioners' sugar.

*Walnut Marionettes:* Substitute ground walnuts for the hazelnuts. Use apricot preserves or apple or currant jelly for the filling and place a walnut half in the center. Sprinkle with confectioners' sugar before serving.

*Praline Marionettes:* Substitute light brown sugar for the granulated sugar and use pecans instead of hazelnuts. Season the dough with 1 teaspoon Praline, the New Orleans liqueur made from pecans. Instead of a filling, press a pecan half in the center of each marionette before baking. Omit the confectioners' sugar.

These marionettes can be made as cookies instead of tarts: prepare them the same way, baking the cookies on greased pastry sheets for about 10 minutes.

## ALMOND CONTESSAS

These Almond Contessas are half cake, half tart, and every bite is tantalizing and calls for another. They are delicate, crisp, and buttery.

You can time them to your convenience, as they freeze well. They are perfect to have in the freezer to bake on short notice for unexpected company. I serve them often for large parties and receptions, and they make a lovely sweet with coffee at the end of a cocktail party or buffet supper.

### CONTESSAS
½ cup (1 stick) unsalted butter, at room temperature
¼ cup sugar
1 large egg yolk
1 cup sifted all-purpose flour
¼ teaspoon salt
1 teaspoon cognac vanilla (see page 29)

### ALMOND FILLING
½ cup sugar
⅓ cup unsalted butter, at room temperature
⅔ cup grated blanched almonds
1 large egg
½ teaspoon pure almond extract
Confectioners' sugar, for dusting

1. Using an electric mixer, cream the butter and sugar together until smooth. Add the egg yolk and beat until fluffy. Blend in the flour, salt, and vanilla. Wrap the dough and place it in the refrigerator to firm up, 30 to 40 minutes.
2. Make the almond filling: with an electric mixer or in a food processor, cream together the sugar and butter until smooth. Add the grated almonds, egg, and almond extract and blend well. (Covered and refrigerated, this filling will keep for several weeks.)

3.   Preheat the oven to 350°F.

4.   Using the cushion of your thumb, press the dough into 15 to 18 tiny (2- or 2½-inch) nonstick tart tins. The dough should be like a fine flaky pie crust dough, a bit thinner around the sides of the tart tins but thick enough at the bottom to hold the almond filling. Put 1 to 2 teaspoons of the filling in the center of each tart.

5.   Put the tart tins on a cookie sheet and bake on the middle rack of the pre-heated oven until lightly browned, 20 to 25 minutes. Allow them to cool and then remove from the tart tins.

6.   Just before serving, dust the Almond Contessas with sifted confectioners' sugar.

Makes 15 to 18 tarts

VARIATIONS:

*Glazed Almond Contessas:* Season apricot preserves with dark rum and spread the glaze over the almond filling before the baked tarts are allowed to cool.

*Pineapple Contessas:* Fill the tarts with pineapple preserves instead of the almond filling.

You can make the Almond Contessas in larger (4- to 7-inch) tart tins. Before serving, sprinkle them with confectioners' sugar and cut into wedges.

You can make Almond Contessas in the morning before a party, but don't hold them for longer than a day—they'll lose their crispness. They freeze very well before baking, however—just place the filled tart tins, covered, in the freezer. When you're ready to serve them, place the still-frozen tarts in a preheated 350°F oven and bake for 25 to 30 minutes. (Both the almond and the pineapple fillings freeze well.)

### BLANCHING ALMONDS

To blanch almonds, place them in boiling water for 2 to 3 minutes. Drain the nuts and as soon as they are cool enough to touch, slip off the skins by squeezing the almonds between your fingers. Spread out the nuts on a baking sheet and allow them to dry.

## MARVELOUS GINGERSNAPS

This gingersnap recipe was given to me by my friend the late Helen McCully, who was the distinguished food editor at *McCall's* and later at *House Beautiful* for many years. Helen was without a doubt the originator of exquisite food photography in fashionable magazines. She was not a photographer herself, but the dream was hers and she carried it through.

*2 cups sifted all-purpose flour*
*1 teaspoon baking powder*
*½ teaspoon baking soda*
*1 teaspoon ground cinnamon*
*1 teaspoon ground cloves*
*½ teaspoon ground allspice*
*1 teaspoon ground ginger*
*6 tablespoons (¾ stick) unsalted butter, at room temperature*
*6 tablespoons solid vegetable shortening*
*1 cup sugar*
*1 large egg*
*¼ cup molasses*
*½ to 1 cup coarse sugar crystals*

1.  Preheat the oven to 375°F. Butter a cookie sheet (or use a nonstick sheet).
2.  In a mixing bowl, combine the flour, baking powder, baking soda, and spices. Stir together thoroughly and set aside.
3.  With an electric mixer or in a food processor, cream together the butter, shortening, and sugar until smooth. Add the egg and molasses and mix thoroughly.
4.  Stir the flour mixture into the butter mixture and beat until well blended (but don't overbeat or the cookies will be tough).
5.  Sprinkle the sugar crystals on a work surface. Roll teaspoonfuls of the dough between your palms to form 1-inch balls. Roll the balls in the sugar crystals and place them 2½ to 3 inches apart on the prepared baking sheet. Press down on them slightly with your hand.
6.  Bake on the middle rack of the preheated oven for about 15 minutes or until firm but not brown on the top or the bottom. Let the cookies cool on the baking sheet for a minute or so and then transfer them to racks or foil to cool completely. As soon as they have cooled, store them in an airtight container or freeze them.

Makes about 50 cookies

> Don't try to make these gingersnaps in hot, humid weather—they won't be crisp.

## MINCEMEAT TURNOVERS

Long before our first Thanksgiving in New England, mincemeat was an integral part of the Christmas feast in the British Isles. The mincemeat process was used at first as a way to preserve food but gradually became the basis for many time-honored holiday desserts. Mincemeat pie came first, and it evolved in a number of ways: into cookies, cakes, and tarts. Turnovers are a great favorite, as they are one of the best ways to showcase a special, flaky crust—a small, tantalizing sweet for a holiday tea.

*Double recipe Flaky Butter Pastry dough (see page 50)*
*1 to 2 cups St. Augustine Mincemeat or Marvelous Mincemeat*
*    (see page 229 or 230)*
*Confectioners' sugar, for dusting*

1.  Preheat the oven to 375°F. If you do not have a nonstick baking sheet, grease a regular one very, very lightly.
2.  Roll the dough out ⅛ inch thick and cut out 3- or 3½-inch rounds with a cookie cutter. You should have about 15 rounds.
3.  Put a spoonful (not more than 2 teaspoons) of mincemeat in the center of each round. Dampen the top edge of the round and fold the bottom half of the round up to form a half-moon shape. Crimp the edges together with a fork and poke a few air vents in the top with the fork.
4.  Bake the turnovers until they are light golden brown, 15 to 18 minutes. Cool them on racks. Just before serving, dust them with confectioners' sugar.

Makes about 15 turnovers

These turnovers can be frozen, baked or unbaked, several weeks ahead of time. Heat already-baked turnovers (without thawing them) in a preheated 375°F oven for 15 to 20 minutes. Unbaked frozen turnovers will take 35 to 40 minutes in a preheated 375°F oven.

## KATHY'S DRIED CHERRY SCONES

I doubt if there ever existed a more delicious English scone. The dried cherries, of course, make them very special, but it's the balance of the ingredients that sets the scones apart. This is, of course, true in all fine baking.

Kathy Cary is one of Louisville's leading chefs. She has been invited to stage dinners at the James Beard House in New York—to great acclaim and flying colors.

½ cup sun-dried cherries
2 tablespoons plus 2¼ cups sifted all-purpose flour
½ teaspoon salt
2 teaspoons baking powder
1 teaspoon baking soda
Zest of ½ lemon
Zest of ½ navel orange
½ cup sugar
6 tablespoons (¾ stick) unsalted butter, chilled and cut into small pieces
2 large eggs
1 tablespoon cold water
2 teaspoons pure vanilla extract or cognac vanilla (see page 29)
1½ cups sour cream
Salt

1. Preheat the oven to 400°F. Lightly butter a baking sheet (or use a nonstick baking sheet).
2. Toss the cherries with the 2 tablespoons flour and set them aside.
3. In a mixing bowl, combine the 2¼ cups flour with the salt, baking powder, and baking soda.
4. Combine the lemon zest, orange zest, and sugar in a food processor and twirl until the zest is finely grated (or grate the zest by hand and add it to the sugar).
5. Cut the butter into the flour mixture as you would for a pie crust; the mixture should be slightly crumbly. Add the zest mixture and combine thoroughly.
6. In a small bowl, whip together 1 of the eggs, the cold water, and the vanilla. Add them to the flour alternately with the sour cream, stirring until the dough is well mixed but still soft (it's a good idea to do this by hand); don't overwork the dough. Gently fold in the cherries.
7. Spoon about 3 tablespoons of the dough onto the prepared baking sheet for each scone. Smooth the top of each scone with a dough scraper or your hand. Stir the remaining egg with a few grains of salt and brush it over the top of each scone.

8. Bake the scones on the middle rack of the preheated oven until they are golden brown, about 20 minutes.

Makes 12 large or 18 small scones

# GINGER ROLL WITH MARRONS

There are few flavors more appropriate for the Christmas season than ginger and chestnuts in all their different presentations. This ginger roll, with marrons (preserved chestnuts) in the whipped cream, is a wonderful surprise for a Christmas tea or fireside picnic—very special indeed! Several weeks before making this recipe, I drain the syrup from the jar of marrons and cover them with cognac.

**CAKE**
⅔ cup sifted all-purpose flour
½ teaspoon baking powder
½ teaspoon baking soda
2½ teaspoons ground ginger
2 teaspoons ground cinnamon
½ teaspoon ground allspice
¼ teaspoon ground cloves
½ teaspoon ground coriander
½ teaspoon salt
4 large eggs, separated
⅔ cup lightly packed light brown sugar
3 tablespoons molasses (sorghum if possible)

**FILLING**
2 tablespoons cognac or brandy
1 cup sliced preserved marrons, marinated in brandy or cognac for several weeks
1 cup heavy or whipping cream, whipped

1.  Preheat the oven to 350°F. Line a 10 × 15-inch jelly roll pan with wax paper, parchment, or aluminum foil, allowing a 1½-inch overhang on all sides. Butter the paper generously.
2.  In a mixing bowl, sift together the flour, baking powder, baking soda, spices, and salt. Set aside.
3.  Using an electric mixer in a large bowl, beat the egg yolks with the brown sugar until thoroughly blended (the mixture will remain slightly grainy). Add the molasses, then stir in the flour mixture.
4.  Whip the egg whites until they hold a stiff peak. Gently fold half the whites into the batter to lighten it. Then fold in the remaining whites.
5.  Spoon the batter into the prepared pan and bake on the middle rack of the preheated oven until the cake springs back at once when lightly touched, 15 to 20 minutes. (Do not allow it to bake until it loosens from the sides of the pan.)
6.  Remove the pan from the oven and cover the cake with very slightly dampened cheesecloth. Allow the cake to cool in the pan.
7.  Lift the paper or foil slightly to loosen the cake from the pan and turn out the cake onto a large piece of foil. Brush the cake with the cognac. Stir the marinated marrons into the whipped cream and spread it generously over the cake. Carefully roll up the cake, jelly roll fashion, using the foil to help you hold it as you roll. Cover the rolled cake with foil and refrigerate until you are ready to serve it (it will keep for 2 or 3 days).
8.  To serve the cake, cut it into ¾-inch-thick slices.

Serves about 20

Don't throw away that marron syrup when you replace it with cognac. Mix the syrup with 1 or 2 tablespoons cognac or brandy and serve it over ice cream.

## THE CHARTWELL CAKE

This is, admittedly, an expensive cake, but it is very elegant and delicious when made with glazed fruit imported from Australia. It is a royal English cake of distinction and probably at its very best served with a fine tea or coffee or a dry Madeira or Spanish sherry. In the latter case, it would probably be best to dust the cake with sifted confectioners' sugar or to use the glaze—forgo the frosting. In any case, do serve very dainty slices.

Calvados is a fine French apple brandy and is one of my favorites!

*1 cup sultana (golden) raisins*
*1 cup chopped glazed pears*
*1 cup chopped glazed apricots*
*1 cup chopped candied pineapple*
*⅓ cup light rum, Calvados, or Spanish sherry*
*1 cup (2 sticks) unsalted butter, at room temperature*
*1¾ cups superfine sugar*
*6 large eggs, separated*
*¼ cup heavy or whipping cream or milk*
*2¾ cups sifted all-purpose flour*
*½ teaspoon salt, sifted with the flour*
*2 teaspoons baking powder*
*¼ cup grated blanched almonds*
*¼ cup slivered almonds*
*¼ cup unsalted pistachio nuts, halved*
*2 teaspoons cognac vanilla (see page 29)*
*Calvados Glaze or Calvados Frosting (recipes follow)*

1.  Twenty-four hours before you plan to bake the cake, combine the fruits with the rum in a bowl and set aside to marinate.

2. Preheat the oven to 300°F. Grease a large tube or bundt pan or several metal loaf pans; line them with heavy-duty aluminum foil.
3. With an electric mixer, cream the butter and 1 cup of the superfine sugar. Add the egg yolks and beat until the mixture is a lighter shade of yellow and is smooth and thick like mayonnaise. Add the cream.
4. Fold in the flour, salt, baking powder, and grated almonds. Then add the slivered almonds, pistachios, cognac vanilla, and marinated fruit with its liqueur. Blend into the batter thoroughly.
5. Beat the egg whites until they hold a soft peak. Add the remaining ¾ cup superfine sugar and beat until they hold a stiff peak. Fold a little of the egg whites into the batter to lighten it; then fold in the rest thoroughly.
6. Spoon the batter into the prepared pan(s) and place on the middle rack of the preheated oven. Bake until the cake springs back at once when touched with your finger or until a cake tester comes out clean. This will take approximately 2 hours, depending on the size of the pan(s).
7. Remove the cake from the oven and allow it to cool for 5 minutes. Then unmold it onto a rack. Brush it with the Calvados Glaze while it is still warm or let it cool thoroughly and then spread it with the Calvados Frosting.

Serves 16 to 18

VARIATION:
You can omit the raisins if you like and substitute a cup of another fruit. French glazed prunes are delicious, and the touch of black is rather beautiful.

If the cake batter looks a bit curdled, fold in an extra tablespoon or two of sifted flour before adding the egg whites.

If you like, you can bake this cake in a sheet-cake pan that has been greased and lined with heavy-duty foil (the baking time will be shorter). Frost the cake and cut it into small pieces—lovely for large teas, receptions, and holiday celebrations.

## CALVADOS GLAZE

*¾ cup sifted confectioners' sugar*
*2 to 3 tablespoons Calvados*

Stir the confectioners' sugar and Calvados together until smooth and brush on the warm cake. (If you used several cake pans, you may need to double the amount of glaze.)

VARIATION:
Instead of the Calvados, you can use Grand Marnier, cognac, or imported French or German kirsch (no substitutes, please).

## CALVADOS FROSTING

*½ cup (1 stick) unsalted butter, at room temperature*
*1 large egg yolk*
*1½ cups sifted confectioners' sugar*
*2 to 3 tablespoons Calvados, cognac, or Grand Marnier*

Cream the butter and the egg yolk with an electric mixer or in a food processor. Add the confectioners' sugar and Calvados and blend until smooth. Spread over the cooled cake.

# A CHRISTMAS LUNCHEON

## MENU 15

Chilled White Wine
*My Favorite Shrimp Salad*
Rosemary Buns or French Baguettes
*Chocolate Pots-de-Crème*
*Tiny Banana Muffins or Dainty Pecan Muffins*
*Williamsburg Bourbon Truffles*
Coffee

The Shrimp Salad should be the *pièce de résistance* of this elegant Christmas luncheon. I hope you will enjoy it so much you will want it again and again.

The finest shrimp in the United States swims in our Southern waters, and it is by far the most beloved of all seafoods. Ken Barry, the owner of the Blue Fin Fish Company in Louisville, is an authority on seafood and fish. As a young man he lived on the *Tina Marie*, a long liner boat in

Folly Beach, South Carolina, for four years as an apprentice to learn about seafood, and his knowledge is vast. Ken says the East Coast white shrimp that swims from North Carolina to the Gulf of Mexico near Texas, and from Cape Hatteras to Cape Canaveral near St. Augustine, Florida, is the four-star shrimp in the United States. The Key West pink shrimp is also good and gets three stars, but the brown shrimp is high in iodine, which gives it a strong flavor and thus makes it not as delicious as the white or pink.

## MY FAVORITE SHRIMP SALAD

The flavor of this salad depends on the quality of the dressing ingredients as much as it does on the freshness of the shrimp. This salad is wonderful served with my Rosemary Buns (see page 138), but French baguettes make a nice alternative to the buns.

*3 cups freshly cooked shrimp*
*½ cup very finely slivered celery*
*2 tablespoons drained capers*
*2 or 3 anchovy fillets, rinsed and chopped*
*6 tablespoons extra-virgin olive oil*
*2 tablespoons white wine tarragon vinegar*
*Salt to taste*
*Fresh lemon juice to taste*
*Cayenne pepper to taste*
*Homemade or good-quality commercial mayonnaise (made without sugar)*
*Pale curly chicory or iceberg lettuce, for serving (optional)*

1.  Devein the shrimp and cut them in half if they are large.
2.  In a large mixing bowl, combine the shrimp, celery, capers, anchovies, oil, and vinegar. Toss thoroughly. Taste for salt; it may not need any extra because of the anchovies. Add salt if needed, lemon juice, and cayenne. Add enough mayonnaise to bind the mixture and toss again.
3.  Serve the salad as is in a beautiful glass bowl or place it on a bed of chicory or iceberg lettuce.

Serves 4 to 6

VARIATION:
*Summer Shrimp Salad:* Stuff ripe tomatoes with the salad and garnish with black Niçoise or ripe California olives.

## CHOCOLATE POTS-DE-CRÈME

divine taste of chocolate for a lovely Christmas luncheon.

*2 cups heavy or whipping cream*
*¼ cup sugar*
*4 ounces dark sweet chocolate (Callebaut, Lindt, or Tobler is best)*
*6 large egg yolks*
*1 teaspoon pure vanilla extract or cognac vanilla (see page 29)*

**WHIPPED CREAM TOPPING**
*1 cup heavy or whipping cream*
*1 tablespoon cognac*
*Sugar to taste*

1. Preheat the oven to 325°F.
2. Combine the 2 cups cream, ¼ cup sugar, and chocolate in the top of a double boiler and place over simmering water. When the chocolate has melted, stir until the mixture is smooth. Remove the pan from the heat and let it cool a bit.
3. Using an electric mixer, beat the egg yolks until they are frothy and have turned a lighter shade of yellow. Beat the yolks into the chocolate mixture. Blend in the vanilla.
4. Pour the mixture into pot-de-crème or custard cups and set them in a shallow baking pan. Add warm water to reach ⅔ of the way up the sides of the cups.
5. Place the pan on the middle rack of the preheated oven and bake until a knife inserted in the center comes out clean, about 1 hour.
6. Remove the cups from the baking pan and refrigerate until well chilled, several hours or as long as overnight.
7. Before serving, prepare the whipped cream topping: beat the cream, cognac, and sugar together until the mixture holds a soft peak. Place a dollop on each cup.

Serves 6 to 8

# TINY BANANA MUFFINS

Tiny Banana Muffins are a delight served warm with fruit sherbet or ice cream. They can be made ahead and warmed at serving time. The contrast of a warm muffin with cold fruit sherbet is wonderful.

½ cup (1 stick) unsalted butter, at room temperature
1½ cups sugar
2 large eggs
2 cups sifted all-purpose flour
2½ teaspoons baking powder
½ teaspoon salt
¼ teaspoon baking soda
¼ cup buttermilk
2 large bananas, not too ripe
1½ teaspoons pure vanilla extract or cognac vanilla (see page 29),
    or 1 tablespoon Cointreau
⅓ cup confectioners' sugar, sifted, for dusting

1. Preheat the oven to 375°F. Butter 2 muffin tins that have 12 very small muffin cups each (or use nonstick muffin tins).
2. Using an electric mixer or food processor, cream the butter and sugar together thoroughly. Add the eggs and beat until the mixture is smooth and creamy; it should look like mayonnaise.
3. Sift the flour, baking powder, and salt together into a mixing bowl.
4. In a small bowl, add the baking soda to the buttermilk and stir until dissolved. In another bowl, mash the bananas with a fork (you should have 1 cup). Immediately add the buttermilk and soda to the mashed bananas (this will keep the bananas from darkening). Stir in the vanilla.
5. Alternating, add the flour mixture and the banana mixture to the egg mixture. Blend well but work fast to keep the bananas from darkening.
6. Spoon the batter into the muffin tins, filling each cup ¾ full. Bake on the middle rack of the preheated oven until the muffins are a light golden brown and a cake tester inserted in the center comes out clean, 20 to 25 minutes (the exact timing depends on the size of the muffin cups that are used).
7. Remove the muffins from the tins. Just before serving, dust them with confectioners' sugar.

Makes 24 tiny muffins

If you don't have the tiny muffin tins, this recipe will make 12 to 15 medium-size muffins. The tiny muffins have more charm, however.

The buttermilk and soda help prevent the bananas from turning dark. A fine banana bread, cake, or muffin should be yellow, not black.

Use bananas that are yellow and have no brown flecks, as those with flecks are too ripe. Really ripe bananas make a dark banana cake, bread, or muffin.

## DAINTY PECAN MUFFINS

These flavorful nut muffins are especially delicious for afternoon tea or after supper with coffee. Made in small muffin cups, they are exquisite with caramel or coffee ice cream. Hickory nuts, hazelnuts, or walnuts may be substituted for the pecans. This recipe, however, is designed to use pecans. Lovely for a Christmas tea.

2¼ cups sifted all-purpose flour
2½ teaspoons baking powder
½ teaspoon salt
1 cup (2 sticks) unsalted butter, at room temperature
2 cups sugar
4 large eggs
¾ cup milk
1 to 1½ cups chopped pecans
1 teaspoon pure vanilla extract or cognac vanilla (see page 29),
    or 1 tablespoon cognac

1.  Preheat the oven to 375°F. Butter 2 or 3 muffin tins with tiny cups (or use nonstick tins).
2.  Measure the flour into a mixing bowl and add the baking powder and salt. Stir together well and set aside.

3. Using an electric mixer or food processor, cream the butter and sugar together thoroughly. Add the eggs and beat until the mixture is smooth and creamy, resembling mayonnaise.
4. Alternating, blend the flour and the milk into the egg mixture. Add the pecans with a whisk or a spatula. Stir in the vanilla.
5. Spoon the batter into the muffin tins, filling each cup not more than ¾ full. Place the tins on the middle rack of the preheated oven and bake until the muffins are a very light golden brown, about 20 to 25 minutes (the exact time will vary from oven to oven). A cake tester inserted in the center of a muffin should come out clean. Remove the muffins from the tins immediately.

Makes about 30 tiny muffins

If you don't have the muffin tins with tiny cups, this recipe will make about 18 medium-size muffins.

My tiny Ekco brand tins hold about 1½ tablespoons of the batter in each cup.

## WILLIAMSBURG BOURBON TRUFFLES

Bourbon has a great affinity for chocolate. However, no alcohol can be added to *pure* chocolate, as the chocolate will harden beyond repair. When using alcohol in making chocolate candies, frostings, and so on, you may first combine the alcohol with the cream before adding it to the chocolate, or you may combine the chocolate with the cream before adding the alcohol. The French call the combination of chocolate and cream a *ganache*, and it's the base of many candies—especially truffles.

*8 ounces dark semisweet chocolate (Callebaut, Lindt, Tobler, or any*
*    fine imported chocolate)*
*½ cup heavy or whipping cream*
*1½ tablespoons best-quality aged Kentucky bourbon*
*Unsweetened cocoa powder or shaved chocolate sprinkles, for rolling*

1. Break the chocolate into small pieces and combine them with the cream in the top of a double boiler. Place over simmering (not boiling) water and stir until the chocolate has melted and the mixture is smooth.
2. Remove the pan from the heat and allow it to cool slightly, then stir in the bourbon.
3. Pour the mixture into a small bowl, cover it with foil, and refrigerate overnight (or for several days if desired).
4. When you are ready to make the candy, line a baking sheet with aluminum foil. Working quickly, form teaspoonfuls of the chilled ganache into balls. (You want to keep the mixture from softening too much, so use your fingertips rather than the palms of your hands.) As you form the truffles, place them on the foil. Cover the truffles lightly with wax paper or aluminum foil (not plastic wrap—it will make them sticky, as it draws moisture) and leave them in the refrigerator for several hours, or overnight if desired.
5. Sprinkle a pastry sheet with cocoa powder and roll each ball in it, covering it well. Refrigerate the truffles at once and leave until they are quite firm, several hours or as long as overnight.
6. Serve the truffles very cold—in silver or paper fluted cups. It's a charming way to present them.

Makes 24 truffles

These delicious truffles will keep for several weeks in an airtight container in the refrigerator.

   The bourbon should be an aged, superior whiskey. Vanilla is often a secret ingredient in Kentucky's fine bourbons.

# Menus for Ringing in the New Year

## Menu 16

Champagne, Chilled White Wine
*Creole Shrimp with Rice*
Bibb Lettuce Salad with Dijon Vinaigrette Dressing
French Bread
*New Orleans Madeleines*
*Light Opera Soufflé*
Coffee

What better way is there to ring in the new year than the way they often do in New Orleans? Down in Louisiana, they celebrate in style—with creole shrimp, French bread, divine madeleines, and chocolate soufflé!

## CREOLE SHRIMP WITH RICE

reole Shrimp is a beloved recipe in New Orleans, where they have divine shrimp. Mushrooms were not added in the older recipes simply because Louisiana was too far south—mushrooms like cold weather. Now, with refrigeration and air cargo available, mushrooms are often added, and they are a worthy addition.

The sauce, including mushrooms if you like, can be made a couple of days ahead and refrigerated, but *do not* add the shrimp until the last 3 minutes before serving. Overcooking toughens most seafood, especially shrimp.

*12 to 15 ripe tomatoes, peeled and seeded,*
*    or 2 pounds canned peeled Italian tomatoes*
*6 tablespoons extra-virgin olive oil*
*½ cup chopped onions*
*3 ribs celery*
*3 carrots, peeled and cut in half*
*1⅔ cups homemade chicken or veal stock*
*Bouquet garni: 2 imported bay leaves,*
*    6 sprigs fresh French thyme or 1½*
*    teaspoons dried thyme, several sprigs*
*    fresh parsley, and 2 allspice berries,*
*    in a cheesecloth bag*
*1 cup dry white wine*
*½ to 1 small hot red pepper, dried or fresh*
*    (optional)*
*Salt and freshly ground white pepper to taste*
*Cayenne pepper to taste*
*2 cups chopped seeded red bell pepper*
*¾ cup chopped seeded green bell pepper*
*1 tablespoon tomato paste, if needed*

Ring out the old, ring
   in the new,
Ring, happy bells, across
   the snow:
The year is going, let him
   go;
Ring out the false, ring in
   the true.

—Alfred, Lord
   Tennyson

*2 pounds large or jumbo shrimp, peeled and deveined*
*3 tablespoons unsalted butter*
*Chopped fresh parsley, for garnish*
*Hot buttered rice, for serving*

1. Chop the tomatoes coarsely by hand or in a food processor. Pour them, with their juice, into a large saucepan and add the olive oil, onions, celery, and carrots. Bring to a boil and simmer for about 5 minutes.
2. Add the stock and the bouquet garni. Simmer for about 20 minutes. Then add the wine and red pepper and cook for a few minutes longer. Season with salt, white pepper, and cayenne.
3. When the sauce has begun to develop a good flavor, remove the celery, carrots, and bouquet garni. Add the bell peppers and simmer for 5 minutes (you want them to remain somewhat crisp). Add the tomato paste if the tomatoes are not fully flavored and the sauce is too bland and simmer for another 3 to 4 minutes.
4. Add the shrimp and cook no longer than 2 to 3 minutes (the exact time depends upon the size of the shrimp). Blend in the butter and correct the seasoning if necessary.
5. Do not allow the mixture to cook further. If necessary, place the saucepan in a larger pot of warm water, double boiler–style, to keep it warm. Garnish with chopped parsley and serve over hot buttered rice.

Serves 4 to 6

VARIATION:
*Shrimp Creole with Mushrooms:* Sauté ½ pound sliced large mushrooms and add them to the sauce along with the shrimp. Dried porcini or wild Oregon mushrooms add great flavor.

Shrimp that are shelled and deveined before cooking have a more delicate flavor than shrimp that are cooked first, then shelled.

Bouquet garni is a group of herbs and vegetables tied together in a little bundle or fagot. The herbs used nearly always include French thyme, parsley, and imported bay leaf. For certain kinds of soups and other dishes, the aromatic bouquets are made containing other scented vegetables such as celery or a small carrot, or more herbs such as French tarragon, basil, or rosemary. The bouquets are removed from the dishes before serving.

## NEW ORLEANS MADELEINES

Madeleines are one of the most beloved of all the French confections that were brought to New Orleans in the early days. They were always served in the tea shops and gardens of the French Quarter.

Divine as they are, madeleines' hours of perfection are few. They must be eaten the day they come from the oven to be at their most beguiling. The batter, however, will hold in the refrigerator, so they need not be baked all at once.

For the Christmas holiday or to ring in the new year, I add 3 tablespoons finely chopped Australian glazed lemon peel along with the fresh zest. Lemon is an exquisitely refreshing flavor.

¾ cup (1½ sticks) unsalted butter
3 large eggs
⅔ cup sugar
1¼ cups sifted all-purpose or cake flour
Pinch of salt
2 teaspoons grated lemon zest
1 teaspoon pure vanilla extract or cognac vanilla (see page 29)
3 to 4 tablespoons unsalted butter, melted
Confectioners' sugar, for dusting (optional)

1. Preheat the oven to 350°F.

2.  Clarify the ¾ cup butter (this will make a crisper madeleine): place the butter in a heatproof glass pitcher and set it in a saucepan of hot water. Bring the water to a boil and simmer until the fat in the butter has separated from the milky whey, which will settle to the bottom. Set the pitcher aside.
3.  In a bowl, beat the eggs and sugar with an electric mixer until they change to a lighter shade of yellow and fall in ribbons from a spoon.
4.  Fold the flour into the egg mixture. Add the salt, lemon zest, and vanilla. Gently pour the clarified butter into the batter, being careful not to include any of the milky whey. Blend in the butter thoroughly (otherwise it may sink to the bottom of the batter).
5.  Heavily coat madeleine molds with the 3 to 4 tablespoons melted butter. Spoon the batter into the molds, filling them ¾ full. Place the molds on the middle rack of the preheated oven and bake until the madeleines are a light golden brown, 20 to 30 minutes.
6.  Repeat, washing the molds and drying them well each time, until the batter is used up.
7.  Serve cool. If you like, sift confectioners' sugar over the madeleines just before serving them.

Makes 36 madeleines

## LIGHT OPERA SOUFFLÉ

A truly light and delicate chocolate dessert—not too rich, and very charming served in a chafing dish for an intimate and exquisite supper.

3 ounces semisweet chocolate
1 teaspoon ground cinnamon
Tiny pinch of salt
3 tablespoons sugar

¾ cup heavy or whipping cream
3 tablespoons Cointreau, Grand Marnier, brandy, or cognac
3 large eggs, separated
1 teaspoon pure vanilla extract or cognac vanilla (see page 29)
Confectioners' sugar, for dusting
1 cup whipped cream seasoned to taste with Cointreau, Grand Marnier,
    or cognac, for serving

1.  Combine the chocolate, cinnamon, salt, sugar, cream, and Cointreau in the top of a double boiler and place over simmering water. Stir until the mixture is smooth.
2.  Beat the egg yolks slightly in a small bowl and add a little of the melted chocolate mixture to temper them. Then stir the yolk mixture into the remaining chocolate mixture.
3.  Beat the egg whites until they are stiff but not dry. Fold them into the chocolate mixture and add the vanilla.
4.  Spoon the mixture into the blazer of a chafing dish. Pour boiling water into the lower compartment and place the blazer over it. Cover and cook, without uncovering, for 25 minutes.
5.  Remove the cover and let the soufflé cool a bit. Sprinkle it with confectioners' sugar and serve with the seasoned whipped cream.

Serves 4

You can cook this soufflé in a double boiler. Keep the water at a boil and don't lift the lid until the 25 minutes are up. You can also cook it in a buttered and sugared soufflé dish set in a pan of warm water in a 350°F oven.

The recipe can be doubled.

## MENU 17

Champagne, Chilled White Wine, or Red Wine
*Small Grilled Mushroom Sandwiches*
*Beggar's Oysters in Beer Batter*
*Louisiana Oyster Gumbo*
French Bread
*Glacéed Nuts*
*Floating Island*
*Chocolate Lebkuchen*
Coffee

Oysters and champagne! What a wonderful way to ring in the new year. Scholars have written whole books about the oyster, and poets as well as cooks have sung its praises. The oyster's enduring charm is, of course, its unique flavor and succulence. It is one of the most delicious and appetizing foods on earth.

Oysters are a mollusk of antiquity. They were even praised in the cookbooks of ancient Rome. As in cooking all seafood, the shock of intense and prolonged heat will toughen oysters. Treat them tenderly and, of course, they must be fresh.

## SMALL GRILLED MUSHROOM SANDWICHES

G rilled mushroom is one of the easiest, most delectable sandwiches I know. When making them for cocktail parties or for tea, chop the mushrooms in rather small pieces, sauté them in butter, and spread them on fresh white bread (crusts trimmed off). Then roll them up into dainty sandwiches, brush them all over with melted butter, and if you like, cover with foil and refrigerate overnight. When you're ready to serve them, preheat the oven to 425° F and toast away. The charming little rolls will toast evenly all over without turning them. Serve hot to a happy holiday crowd.

*½ pound fresh mushrooms*
*4 tablespoons (½ stick) unsalted butter*
*2 teaspoons peanut or vegetable oil*
*Salt and freshly ground black pepper to taste*
*1 tablespoon chopped fresh parsley*
*8 slices white sandwich bread*
*6 tablespoons (¾ stick) unsalted butter, melted*

1. Rinse the mushrooms quickly under cold running water and brush them clean with a *soft* mushroom brush. Dry them on paper towels and slice them ¼ inch thick, discarding the stems.
2. Heat the 4 tablespoons butter and the oil in a wok or skillet (not cast-iron), add the mushrooms, and stir-fry for no longer than 2 minutes. The mushrooms should remain crisp and should not brown at all. If they give off a lot of juice, drain them and start over with a little butter in a heavy pan. (Refrigerate the buttery mushroom broth to use later in another dish.)
3. Salt and pepper the mushrooms and sprinkle the parsley over them.
4. Spread the mushrooms generously over 4 slices of the bread and top with the remaining slices.

5. Lay the sandwiches on a pastry sheet and brush the top and bottom of each one with the melted butter. (You can wrap the sandwiches in foil at this point and refrigerate them for an hour or so.)
6. Heat a griddle or skillet until it is quite hot but not smoking. Brown the sandwiches on one side; then turn them with a metal spatula and brown the other side, 6 to 8 minutes in all.
7. Cut the sandwiches in half or in thirds and serve hot.

Makes 8 to 12 sandwiches

If you're making a larger number of sandwiches and don't want to cook them in a skillet, preheat the oven to 450°F. Place the sandwiches on a baking sheet and toast in the oven until light golden brown, about 8 minutes.

Avoid cast-iron skillets for this recipe; mushrooms turn almost black when cooked in them.

## BEGGAR'S OYSTERS IN BEER BATTER

I n England in the early eighteenth century, oysters were so plentiful that beggars gathered them and sold them—a dozen for a penny! They were fried in beer batter at the pubs. Many good things never change. (I am speaking of the flavor, of course, not the price!)

### BEER BATTER
2 cups sifted all-purpose flour
1⅛ teaspoons salt, or to taste
1½ tablespoons vegetable oil, extra-virgin olive oil,
    or melted unsalted butter
1 large whole egg
2 large eggs, separated

¾ cup beer
⅔ cup milk

Oil for deep-frying
2 pints large fresh oysters
Lemon wedges, for garnish
Watercress or parsley sprigs, for garnish
Horseradish Mayonnaise (recipe follows), for serving

1. Combine the flour, salt, oil, whole egg, egg yolks, beer, and milk in a blender, food processor, or mixer bowl. Blend until smooth. Cover and refrigerate for 1 to 2 hours.
2. When you are ready to cook the oysters, whip the egg whites until they form stiff peaks. Fold them into the batter. The batter should be fairly thick; add a little milk if it seems too thick (all batters thicken while resting).
3. Heat 3 to 4 inches of oil in a deep-fat fryer until it reaches 375°F.
4. Drain the oysters well on paper towels or a clean cloth. Dip each oyster in the batter, coating it well. As you coat the oysters, arrange them on a shallow plate.
5. Drop the oysters, a few at a time, into the hot oil and cook until golden brown, approximately 2 to 3 minutes. Do not crowd them in the pan. Remove the oysters when they are done and set them on a pastry sheet lined with paper towels. Set the pastry sheet in a warm oven with the door open while you cook the remaining oysters.
6. Serve the oysters on a heated platter, garnished with lemon wedges and watercress. Pass the Horseradish Mayonnaise.

Serves 6 to 8

The slight fermentation of the beer makes a light batter, and the sharp taste of the beer disappears in the frying, but if you prefer, you can substitute milk for the beer. If you do use all milk, add 1½ teaspoons baking powder to replace the leavening power of the beer.

## HORSERADISH MAYONNAISE

Fresh horseradish is now available in most produce markets throughout the United States. If you can't find fresh horseradish, however, try to find a quality bottled horseradish that is plain grated horseradish seasoned with vinegar and salt only, not with milk or sour cream.

*1 cup good-quality mayonnaise*
*1½ tablespoons freshly ground horseradish, or to*
*   taste (see owl, below)*
*Salt to taste*

Combine the mayonnaise, horseradish, and salt. Mix well and store in a closed jar in the refrigerator.

Makes 1 cup

"A loaf of bread," the
   Walrus said,
"Is what we chiefly need;
Pepper and vinegar besides
Are very good indeed—
Now, if you're ready,
   Oysters, dear,
We can begin to feed."

—Lewis Carroll

To make your own horseradish, rinse and peel 1 or 2 medium-size pieces of freshly dug horseradish. Chop into small cubes and place in a food processor with enough cider vinegar to cover. Process until quite finely ground.

Horseradish does not age well, even when refrigerated, as it turns dark and should then be discarded.

## LOUISIANA OYSTER GUMBO

Oysters in all their glory and elegance have been a source of great pride in New Orleans, and in Louisiana in general. Their gumbos are among the South's most famous dishes, and rightfully so.

The word *gumbo* is African and means okra, but not all gumbos contain okra. Okra does thicken soups tastefully—and far better, in my opinion, than filé powder, which was first made by the Indians from sassafras root and has been used extensively. But that, of course, is a matter of personal taste.

Oysters are at their firmest and most delicious in midwinter, and they do make elegant holiday fare. Serve some French bread with this gumbo.

1 frying chicken (3½ to 4 pounds), cut in half
Salt to taste
2 tablespoons unsalted butter, at room
    temperature
2½ quarts water
1½ cups chopped scallions (green onions),
    white bulbs only, or 1½ cups peeled and
    chopped mild onion
4 tablespoons all-purpose flour
½ cup (1 stick) unsalted butter
Bouquet garni: 2 ribs celery, a sprig of fresh thyme
    or a generous pinch of dried thyme, 3 parsley sprigs,
    and 2 imported bay leaves, tied together or in a cheesecloth bag
4 fresh tomatoes, peeled, or 3 best-quality canned tomatoes, chopped or puréed
½ cup chopped green bell pepper
1 large red bell pepper, cored, seeded, and chopped
½ teaspoon dried red pepper flakes, or to taste
1 pound fresh or frozen okra, coarsely chopped

1 medium-size piece of ham bone, ham hock, or thick slice of
    uncooked ham (½ pound), preferably country ham
1 to 1½ pounds small fresh shrimp, shelled and deveined
1 pint fresh oysters with their juice
Tabasco sauce to taste
About 6 cups freshly cooked long-grain rice, for serving
Chopped fresh parsley, for garnish

1. Preheat the oven to 425°F.
2. Arrange the chicken in a shallow roasting pan and season it with salt. Spread the 2 tablespoons butter over the chicken and roast until it is a light golden brown.
3. Transfer the chicken and its cooking juices to a large heavy pot (leave the oven on). Add the water and scallions and bring to a boil. Simmer uncovered until the chicken is tender, 40 to 60 minutes.
4. In the meantime, spread the flour in a pie plate and place in the oven until it is a golden brown (watch it carefully). Melt the ½ cup butter in a heavy saucepan. Add the browned flour, blend, and cook to make a brown roux.
5. Lift the tender chicken halves from the stock and set them aside. Add the roux to the stock, beating hard to blend it in. Add the bouquet garni and bring the stock to a boil. Cook until the roux is thoroughly blended with the stock, 20 to 25 minutes.
6. Add the tomatoes, bell peppers, red pepper flakes, okra, and ham. Simmer until the stock tastes delicious, 30 to 40 minutes, or longer if needed.
7. Remove the ham bone or hock and the bouquet garni. If you used a ham slice, remove it and cut it into small pieces; return the meat to the pot. Remove the chicken meat from the bones and add it to the stock. Cook for at least 5 minutes to blend the flavors. (You can set aside or freeze the base at this point if you like.)
8. Just before serving, add the shrimp and oysters with their juice. Cook gently for no more than 3 or 4 minutes. Add a few drops of Tabasco and salt to taste. If the gumbo is too thick, add a little boiling water (it should be liquid enough to eat with a spoon).

9.  To serve, spoon hot rice into warm soup plates and ladle the gumbo over the rice. Sprinkle with chopped parsley.

Serves 6 to 8

VARIATION:
When you add the shrimp and oysters, stir in ½ to 1 pound fresh lump crab-meat—a delectable addition.

## GLACÉED NUTS

These glacéed nuts add a charming note to the holiday tea table, or they can be offered for a taste of crunchy sweetness with coffee. Neither pecans nor hazelnuts need to be blanched or toasted to be glacéed, but almonds should be blanched and crisped.

*2 to 3 cups large pecan halves, almonds, or hazelnuts*
*2 cups sugar*
*1 cup water*
*Tiny pinch of salt*
*⅓ teaspoon cream of tartar*

1.  If you are using almonds, blanch them first. Then bake them in a 275°F oven for 25 to 30 minutes until they are crisp (watch them carefully). Pecans and hazelnuts do not need to be blanched or toasted.
2.  Combine the sugar, water, salt, and cream of tartar in a heavy nonreactive saucepan. Bring to a boil, cover the pan, and cook for 3 minutes to dissolve the sugar crystals that collect on the sides of the pan. Uncover the pan and cook until the syrup turns a very light amber and registers 280°F on a candy thermometer, 6 to 8 minutes.
3.  Immediately place the saucepan in a larger pan of cold water to stop the cooking. Place the larger pan over a low heat so the syrup will stay liquid.

4.  Dip the nuts, about ¼ cup at a time, into the syrup. Stir them around quickly, then remove them with a slatted spoon and spread them out on a pastry sheet, separating them as best you can. Allow the nuts to dry and harden, 30 to 40 minutes.
5.  Store the nuts in an airtight tin. Don't refrigerate them or they will become sticky.

Makes 2 to 3 cups

VARIATION:
Instead of separating the nuts, you can make nut clusters by allowing the nuts to stay in groups of three or four while they dry. After they cool, go one step further: dip them in melted semisweet or dark sweet chocolate. Tobler, Lindt, and Callebaut semisweet chocolate are the best.

# FLOATING ISLAND

One of the favorite wintertime or holiday desserts. The meringue can be made a day ahead, as can the custard. Freeze or refrigerate the meringue in an airtight container until a few hours before serving.

**CUSTARD**
*3 cups whole milk*
*6 large egg yolks*
*⅔ cup sugar*
*1 teaspoon all-purpose flour*
*1 tablespoon cognac or Grand Marnier*
*2 large egg whites*

**MERINGUE**
*4 large egg whites*
*½ cup sugar*
*½ teaspoon pure vanilla extract or cognac vanilla (see page 29)*
*⅓ cup slivered unsalted pistachios or toasted almonds, for garnish*

1. Pour the milk into a heavy saucepan and, over a medium heat, bring it almost to the boiling point (but do not let it boil). Remove the pan from the heat.
2. Combine the egg yolks and sugar in a mixing bowl and, using an electric mixer, beat until the mixture is light and fluffy. Add the flour and beat again.
3. Slowly pour some of the warm milk into the egg mixture, beating it in well. Then pour the egg mixture into the remaining warm milk. Pour the entire mixture into the top of a double boiler and cook over simmering water until the custard is thick enough to coat a wooden spoon, 3 to 4 minutes.
4. Immediately remove the pan from the heat and stir in the cognac. Pour the custard into a cool dish and refrigerate it until thoroughly chilled, 2 to 3 hours.
5. Beat the 2 egg whites until they form stiff peaks. Fold them into the chilled custard and pour the custard into an attractive shallow serving bowl.
6. Preheat the oven to 275°F.
7. Prepare the meringue: beat the egg whites until they form soft peaks. Very gradually add the sugar, beating continually until the whites hold a stiff peak. Add the vanilla.
8. Butter a ring mold and sprinkle it well with sugar. Spoon the egg whites into the mold and place the mold in a baking pan filled with warm water. Place the pan in the preheated oven and cook until the meringue is firm, about 1 hour. Remove the mold from the baking pan and allow the meringue to cool in the mold.
9. Free the cooled meringue from the sides of the mold with a sharp knife. Turn it out, with the white underside up, into the bowl of custard. Sprinkle the top of the meringue with the pistachios. Leave the meringue in the custard for 1 hour before serving (this softens the meringue).

10.  To serve, spoon some of the custard into each dessert bowl and top with a scoop (an "island") of meringue.

Serves 6

VARIATION:
Add ½ cup ground blanched almonds to the meringue's egg whites before cooking them.

> Don't worry if the meringue browns a bit in the oven, or if it seems a little hard. It will soften up nicely in the custard.

## CHOCOLATE LEBKUCHEN

*L*ebkuchen means "lively cake" in German. You can enliven yours with fruits and nuts and your favorite liqueur if you wish.

1½ teaspoons ground cinnamon
½ teaspoon ground cloves
½ teaspoon ground allspice
1 teaspoon ground coriander
¾ cup (1½ sticks) unsalted butter, at room temperature
¾ cup granulated sugar
¾ cup firmly packed light brown sugar
3 large eggs
1 teaspoon cognac vanilla (see page 29) or 1 tablespoon cognac or brandy
2 cups sifted all-purpose flour
1½ teaspoons baking powder
1 teaspoon regular or coarse (kosher) salt
6 ounces imported dark bittersweet chocolate, melted
Confectioners' sugar, for dusting

1. Preheat the oven to 350°F. Lightly grease a 10½ × 15-inch rimmed pastry sheet and set it aside.
2. Combine the spices on a piece of wax paper or aluminum foil, stirring them together well.
3. Using an electric mixer, cream the butter and both sugars together well. Add the eggs and beat until the mixture is as smooth and creamy as mayonnaise. Stir in the vanilla.
4. In a mixing bowl, stir together the flour, baking powder, salt, and spice mixture. Add them to the egg mixture, beating them in quickly but thoroughly (don't overbeat or the cake will be dry).
5. Add the melted chocolate, stirring it in thoroughly.
6. Spread the batter out on the prepared pastry sheet and bake on the middle rack of the preheated oven for about 25 minutes or until the cake springs back to the touch. Do not overbake the cake.
7. Allow the cake to cool on the sheet and then cut it into squares. Just before serving, sprinkle confectioners' sugar over the top.

Makes about 48 squares

VARIATION:
For a Christmas treat: while it is still hot, brush the cooked cake with brandy, cognac, or Grand Marnier. Cut the cake into rounds and sprinkle with confectioners' sugar. Don't stew over the offal—small and grown-up children love it!

## MENU 18

Champagne, Chilled White Wine, or Red Wine
*Warm Duck Salad on Mesclun*
*Good Fortune Tea Cake*
*Frozen Vanilla Soufflé*
*Kentucky Colonels*
Demitasse

This is a very special menu—one of my great favorites. The Warm Duck Salad is delicious and the Good Fortune Tea Cake is not only wonderful to eat but lots of fun for everyone, old and young. You'll see!

## WARM DUCK SALAD ON MESCLUN

The East and the West meet in this divine warm salad. Served on mesclun, it is a very special holiday lunch or supper. Tangerine ice or sherbet with Chinese cookies and demitasse will make a memorable meal, and it deserves to be served with champagne or a dry white or red wine.

4 boneless duck breasts (about 1½ pounds)
½ cup soy sauce
3 tablespoons thinly sliced pickled ginger (available at gourmet and Asian markets)
Juice of 1 lemon
6 scallions (green onions), white bulbs and ½ inch green stems, chopped
2 tablespoons imported sesame oil
1½ tablespoons vegetable oil
3 tablespoons unsalted butter
4 to 6 cups mesclun (tiny mixed lettuces such as tender Bibb, slivered endive, and watercress leaves)
Red bell pepper, sliced into thin rings, or edible flowers, for garnish

1. Skin the duck breasts and trim off as much fat as possible. Slicing across the grain, cut the meat into thin strips.
2. In a large nonmetallic bowl, stir together the soy sauce, pickled ginger, lemon juice, scallions, and sesame oil. Add the duck and toss to cover well. Cover the bowl and refrigerate for at least 1 hour or as long as 4 hours.
3. Drain the duck, reserving the marinade.
4. Heat the vegetable oil in a wok or skillet. When it is quite hot, add the duck and stir-fry until tender, about 3 minutes. Remove the duck and keep warm.
5. Add the marinade to the wok. If there seems to be a surplus, cook the marinade to reduce it a bit. Then add the butter gradually, stirring it into the sauce. Taste for seasoning.
6. Return the duck to the wok and cook it for 3 minutes to rewarm it.

7. Divide the mesclun among 4 salad plates and spoon the duck and sauce over the lettuces. Garnish with rings of red bell pepper or with edible flowers.

Serves 4

VARIATIONS:
For a heartier salad, place a spoonful of hot white or brown rice on the mesclun and top it with the duck and sauce.

*Warm Chicken Salad:* Substitute chicken breasts for the duck.

 *Mesclun* is French for "mixture"—one of miniature salad greens.

## GOOD FORTUNE TEA CAKE

In the teachings of the ancient Chinese philosopher Confucius, the orange and the almond represent harmony, love, and good fortune. The person who finds the almond in his piece of cake will have harmony and good fortune in the year ahead.

First, however, each guest must look into the small mirror in the center of the cake and make a wish! Only then are the guests given a slice of cake. The cake is yummy . . . but who found the almond? What fun for a holiday tea!

*2 cups sugar*
*Zest of 1 lemon*
*Zest of ½ navel orange*
*1 cup (2 sticks) unsalted butter, at room temperature*
*4 large eggs, separated*
*3 cups sifted all-purpose flour*
*2 teaspoons baking powder*
*⅛ teaspoon salt*

*1 cup milk*
*1 tablespoon fresh lemon juice*
*1½ teaspoons fresh orange juice*
*1½ teaspoons cognac vanilla (see page 29) or 1 tablespoon cognac*
*2 whole blanched almonds*
*2 small mirrors (see owl, next page)*
*Good Fortune Frosting (recipe follows)*
*Small edible flowers, for garnish*

1. Preheat the oven to 350°F. Butter two 8½-inch springform pans and dust them with flour. Shake out the excess flour and set the pans aside.
2. Combine the sugar, lemon zest, and orange zest in a food processor and twirl until the zest is finely grated (or grate the zest by hand and add it to the sugar).
3. Using an electric mixer, beat the zest mixture and butter together until thoroughly blended. Add the egg yolks, one at a time, beating until the mixture is smooth and creamy.
4. In another mixing bowl, combine the flour with the baking powder and salt; stir well. Alternating, add the milk and the flour to the egg mixture. Do not overbeat.
5. Add the lemon juice, orange juice, and vanilla and blend carefully.
6. Beat the egg whites until they hold a stiff peak. Gently fold a third of the whites into the batter to lighten it. Then fold in the remaining whites, mixing gently but thoroughly. Pour the batter into the prepared pans and poke an almond down into the batter in each pan.
7. Bake the cakes on the lower rack of the preheated oven until a cake tester inserted in the middle comes out clean, 50 minutes to 1 hour. Watch the cakes carefully—if they overbake they will be dry. Don't let them cook so long that the cake separates from the sides of the pan— that's too long.
8. Allow the cakes to cool in the pans for 5 minutes. Then remove them from the pans and set them on wire racks to cool thoroughly before frosting them.

9. Frost the cakes: place a small mirror in the center of each cake and frost around the edges to seal it in place. Then cover the remaining top and sides of the cakes with the frosting. Place each cake on a stand or platter and arrange a few very small edible flowers around the mirrors.
10. Before serving the cakes, each guest in turn looks into the mirror and makes a wish. The person who finds an almond in his slice will have a year of harmony and good fortune—it's a promise!

Serves 6 to 8 per cake

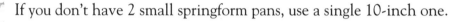

If you don't have 2 small springform pans, use a single 10-inch one.

This is one of the best cakes I know for its "keeping" qualities. Stored in an airtight container, it will stay moist for days.

The tiny mirrors that come in handbags—or at least used to—are a good size: 2 to 3 inches in diameter.

## GOOD FORTUNE FROSTING

½ cup heavy or whipping cream
1 cup (2 sticks) unsalted butter, at room temperature
6 cups sifted confectioners' sugar
¼ teaspoon salt, or to taste
1½ teaspoons good-quality pure almond extract, or more to taste
   (I like Lochhead brand)

1. Heat the cream in a small saucepan until it is warm.
2. Using an electric mixer or food processor, cream the butter, confectioners' sugar, and salt together until smooth. Slowly add the warm cream, beating until smooth. Add the almond extract. If you won't be using the frosting immediately, cover and refrigerate it.

Makes enough for two 8½-inch cakes

To be beautiful on the cake, the frosting must have a smooth spreading consistency. If it is too soft, beat it very hard with an electric mixer to thicken it up. If it is too stiff, add a spoonful of boiling water.

## FROZEN VANILLA SOUFFLÉ

This soufflé is actually a rich and delicious ice cream that does not have to be turned in an ice-cream machine. It is one of the most delightful "do ahead" desserts I know, and it blends exquisitely with all of the holiday dinners. That is the talent of vanilla. It must, of course, be true vanilla and not the imitation, which is worse than no flavoring at all.

Serve this soufflé plain or with a fruit sauce.

*1¼ cups sugar*
*8 large egg yolks*
*2 cups milk*
*Tiny pinch of salt*
*2 teaspoons pure vanilla extract or cognac vanilla (see page 29)*
*3 cups heavy or whipping cream*
*1 to 1½ tablespoons cognac or brandy*
*Unsweetened cocoa powder or chocolate shavings, for garnish*
*Raspberry Sauce or Fresh Pineapple Sauce (recipes follow), for serving*

1.  Place a medium-size stainless-steel bowl in the refrigerator to chill.

2. Using an electric mixer, combine the sugar and egg yolks. Beat until the mixture has turned a lighter shade of yellow and falls in ribbons from a wooden spoon. Add the milk and mix thoroughly.

3. Transfer the mixture to a saucepan and cook it over a medium heat, stirring constantly, until it lightly coats a wooden spoon. *Do not allow the mixture to boil.* Remove the pan from the heat and immediately pour the custard into the cool stainless-steel bowl. Stir in the salt and vanilla and refrigerate, covered, until cold. (To speed things up, you can pour the mixture into a shallow container and place it in the freezer for about 1 hour.)

4. When the custard is chilled, add the cream and cognac and blend well.

5. Tie a foil collar around a 1-quart soufflé dish, letting it extend 3 inches above the rim of the dish. Brush the inside of the collar with vegetable oil.

6. Spoon most of the mixture into the soufflé dish, filling it up to the rim. Place the soufflé in the freezer and leave it until it is rather firm, 3 to 4 hours. Meanwhile, cover the remaining mixture and place it in the refrigerator.

7. When the soufflé is firm, spoon the remaining mixture on top of it and allow it to freeze until frozen hard, another 3 to 4 hours or as long as overnight.

8. Before serving, remove the foil collar and sprinkle the top with sieved cocoa powder to simulate the browned top of a soufflé. Pass the Raspberry Sauce or Fresh Pineapple Sauce.

Serves 6 to 8

## RASPBERRY SAUCE

*2 cups fresh or frozen raspberries*
*3 to 6 tablespoons sugar*
*1 teaspoon fresh lemon juice*

1.  Combine the raspberries, sugar, and lemon juice in a food processor or blender and process until smooth. Serve over ice cream, cakes, puddings, charlottes, and Bavarians.
2.  Store the sauce in a closed jar in the refrigerator. It will keep for a few days.

Makes about 1½ cups

VARIATIONS:
Add 1 to 2 tablespoons framboise (raspberry *eau-de-vie*), or use fresh or frozen strawberries instead of raspberries.

## FRESH PINEAPPLE SAUCE

*1 large ripe pineapple*
*1½ cups sugar*
*Fresh lemon juice to taste*

1.  Trim, peel, and core the pineapple. Cut the fruit into cubes and purée it in a food processor; you should have 2 cups of purée. Add the sugar and process for several minutes for the sugar to dissolve. Taste the sauce and add lemon juice. Taste again and add more sugar if needed (fresh fruit varies in sweetness).
2.  Store the sauce in a closed jar in the refrigerator. It will keep for a few days.

Makes about 1¼ cups

## KENTUCKY COLONELS

The late Ruth Booe of Frankfort, Kentucky, was a beautiful and talented Southern lady who created the now-famous Kentucky Colonel Candy—the candy that has a delicious creamy fondant center delicately flavored with bourbon, a large pecan half in its heart, and a covering of fine imported chocolate.

When Prohibition came along in 1919, Ruth and her partner, Rebecca, could no longer make the bourbon candy for sale, but they continued to make taffy, chocolate fudge, and other sweets in the otherwise unused barroom of the Frankfort Hotel. The old marble counter of the bar was the perfect place to cool and knead their candy. When the Volsted Act was repealed in 1933, Ruth moved the candy business to her home kitchen and Kentucky Colonel Candy again became her best-seller.

The recipe given here is reputed to be Ruth's original one for the first Kentucky Colonel Candy ever made. A worker in Ruth's kitchen secretly gave the recipe to a friend, and thereby began the legacy.

Naturally, over the years and in the ways of man and cooks, the original recipe has been altered, but according to my research on the true origin of this wonderful candy—the way Ruth and Rebecca made it for many years—this is the pristine formula. I give it to you with the blessing of John Booe, who inherited his mother's business and continues to supervise a very prosperous candy enterprise in Frankfort today.

½ cup (1 stick) unsalted butter, at room temperature
1 pound sifted confectioners' sugar
¼ teaspoon salt
¼ cup premium-quality aged bourbon
2 cups large pecan halves
1 pound imported semisweet chocolate, such as Lindt, Callebaut, or Tobler, for coating

1. Using an electric mixer or food processor, cream the butter and confectioners' sugar thoroughly. Add the salt and bourbon and mix well.
2. Using your hands, roll the candy into ¾-ounce (tablespoon-size) balls on a cool work surface, placing a pecan half in the center of each ball. As you work, place the candy balls on a pastry sheet. When finished, cover the pastry sheet with foil and refrigerate for 8 hours or as long as overnight.
3. When the balls have chilled, melt the chocolate in the top of a double boiler set over simmering (never boiling) water; the temperature of the chocolate should not exceed 90°F. Remove the pan from the heat and let the chocolate cool to lukewarm.
4. Spear a candy ball on a fork and dip it into the warm chocolate, turning to coat it well. Lift the candy out of the chocolate and hold it above the pan for a few seconds to let the excess chocolate drip off. Gently scrape the bottom of the ball against the edge of the pan to remove any more excess chocolate (this prevents the chocolate from forming a "platform" under the candy). Using a spatula or the side of a knife, slide the candy onto a pastry sheet lined with aluminum foil or wax paper. Store in the refrigerator. Repeat with the remaining balls. When they have chilled enough to become firm (45 minutes to 1 hour), cover them lightly with foil or wax paper (not plastic wrap). Store the candy in the refrigerator; it will keep for about 6 weeks.

Makes about 1½ pounds

Kentucky, Oh
  Kentucky—
'Mid the blossoms newly
  born;
Where the corn is full of
  kernels
And the Colonels full of
  corn.

—Anonymous

## Menu 19

Champagne
Caviar
*Smoked Salmon Open-Face Sandwiches*
French Bread
Celery Curls, Black and Green Olives, Carrot Sticks
*White Wine Sherbet*
*Chocolate and Vanilla Truffles*
Coffee

O ne new year's menu lingers very vividly in my memory. It was a quiet evening with a small group of close friends and family. We had champagne and caviar and my favorite sandwiches of smoked salmon and lobster. It was elegant but easy, and simply delicious.

As the logs burned low and the room began to cool, we had chocolate truffles and hot coffee. It was a great finale to a lovely evening, and a wonderful overture to another year.

## SMOKED SALMON OPEN-FACE SANDWICHES

S andwiches to serve with champagne and caviar. Can you think of a better way to greet the new year?

*½ pound smoked salmon*
*⅔ cup mayonnaise (made without sugar)*
*1 tablespoon fresh lemon juice, or to taste*
*Cayenne pepper to taste*
*1-pound loaf fine, moist white bread, thinly sliced*
*½ cup (1 stick) unsalted butter, at room temperature*

1. Chop the salmon fairly coarsely (I do this with shears). Mix it lightly with the mayonnaise and lemon juice. Season with cayenne and cover and refrigerate until ready to use (it will keep for several days).
2. Using a cookie or biscuit cutter, cut the bread into rounds. Spread the butter over them and top with the salmon mixture. Serve immediately or cover and refrigerate for a short while. (Once made up, these sandwiches do not keep well.)

Serves 16 or more

VARIATION:
Substitute crayfish, lobster, shrimp, or crabmeat for the salmon.

## WHITE WINE SHERBET

This is a beautiful finale to a fine dinner—light yet satisfying, and full of intriguing flavor.

4 cups water
2 cups sugar
Juice of 4 lemons
Juice of 4 navel oranges
1 bottle semisweet white wine, chilled
Sections of navel oranges, slices of kiwi fruit,
    or sprigs of fresh mint, for garnish

1.  Combine the water and sugar in a saucepan and boil for 2 minutes. Pour the syrup into a stainless-steel bowl and let it cool completely.
2.  Add the juices and wine to the syrup and blend thoroughly. Cover the bowl and place it in the freezer for 8 to 10 hours or overnight (the alcohol in the wine slows the freezing process).
3.  Beat the frozen sherbet hard with an electric hand mixer until it is fluffy. Return it to the freezer for several hours or longer.
4.  One to 2 hours before serving, beat the sherbet hard again until it is fluffy. Return it to the freezer.
5.  Serve in sherbet glasses, garnished with orange sections, kiwi slices, or mint sprigs.

Makes about ½ gallon

The more this sherbet is beaten, the smoother it will be (the beating breaks down the ice crystals). It's even better when made in an ice-cream machine.

## CHOCOLATE AND VANILLA TRUFFLES

Chocolate and Vanilla Truffles and coffee, and maybe a tiny glass of Grand Marnier or cognac to accompany them, ring in the new year in a very glorious way! Sit by a glowing fire and enjoy the fun of being together and sharing wonderful bites of delicious food—surely a happy time!

*1½ cups heavy or whipping cream*
*½ pound imported semisweet chocolate, chopped into pieces*
*1½ tablespoons pure vanilla extract or cognac vanilla (see page 29)*
*1 to 1¼ pounds imported semisweet chocolate, for coating*

1. Combine the cream and chopped chocolate in the top of a double boiler and heat over simmering water, stirring occasionally, until smooth. Remove the pan from the heat and allow the ganache to cool a bit.
2. Stir the vanilla into the ganache. Cover and refrigerate until the ganache is very thick, about 5 hours or as long as overnight.
3. Roll the ganache into small balls, about 1¼ tablespoons each, shaping them roughly to resemble real truffles. Place them on a pastry sheet lined with aluminum foil or wax paper. Freeze for several hours or as long as overnight.
4. When the balls are thoroughly frozen, line 2 pastry sheets with wax paper or aluminum foil and set them aside.
5. Melt the coating chocolate in the top of a double boiler set over simmering (not boiling) water; the temperature of the chocolate should not exceed 90°F. Remove the pan from the heat and let the chocolate cool to luke-warm.

6. Spear a truffle on a fork and dip it into the warm chocolate, turning to coat it well. Lift the truffle out of the chocolate and hold it above the pan for a few seconds to let the excess chocolate drip off. Gently scrape the bottom of the truffle against the edge of the pan to remove any more excess chocolate (this prevents the chocolate from forming a "platform" under the truffle). Using a spatula or the side of a knife, slide the truffle onto a prepared pastry sheet. Store in the refrigerator. Repeat with the remaining truffles. When they have chilled long enough to become firm (after 1 to 1½ hours), cover the truffles lightly with aluminum foil or wax paper (not plastic wrap). Store the truffles in the refrigerator; they will keep for about 6 weeks.

Makes about 36 truffles

VARIATION:
*Deluxe Chocolate and Vanilla Truffles:* Instead of the vanilla, add 2 to 3 tablespoons Grand Marnier, cognac, or Cointreau to the cooled ganache.

 Always make the ganache—the mixture of cream and chocolate—before you add the alcohol; otherwise the chocolate will harden beyond repair.

### TIPS FOR MAKING TRUFFLES

- The most important thing is to use premium-quality ingredients.
- When you are preparing the coating, melt no less than 14 to 16 ounces of chocolate. A smaller amount won't hold the heat adequately for dipping.
- Make sure the pan is perfectly dry when you put the coating chocolate in it to melt. The least spattering of water will turn the coating lumpy and hard.
- Never allow chocolate to get any hotter than 90°F when you are melting it. Stir it often to keep the cocoa butter evenly distributed and to prevent "bloom," the discoloring of the chocolate.

• Best results are achieved when working with cool hands in a cool room (60°F to 65°F). Rainy or humid weather will cause havoc with chocolate dipping.

• A special dipping fork is handy, but not essential.

• When you are ready to dip the truffles, the coating chocolate should not feel warm to your fingers; the best temperature is 86°F to 90°F. If the coating is too warm, it won't harden properly. If it is too cool, it will be hard to handle and will lose its gloss.

• Because truffle fillings and ganaches are soft and creamy, they should be kept cold. Work with small amounts at a time, keeping the remainder refrigerated.

• Avoid wrapping candies and ganache in plastic wrap, since it traps moisture and causes the candy to discolor.

• The ideal way to present truffles as gifts is to place each one in a tiny fluted silver or paper cup made for the purpose (available at candy supply stores) and then fit them in a single layer in an airtight tin.

## ABOUT TRUFFLES

If chocolate candy is a frivolity, it is one we never intend to betray. We bless the Spanish adventurer Cortez, who added a touch of sugar to the bitter drink the Aztecs called *xocolatl*.

The Spaniards kept chocolate a secret for a hundred years, but little by little the good news leaked out. It is recorded in early Spanish histories that the Toltec Indians believed that the cocoa bean was a gift from the gods and that chocolate would be their manna in the afterlife. I am counting on that, too.

All the world loves chocolate, and chocolate truffles are the world's most luscious *trompe l'oeil*. We have no clue as to the name of the clever cook who first created these candies so beautifully camouflaged in the shape of a truffle, but it would be a very safe bet that he was a Frenchman, and from truffle country.

In contrast to most hand-dipped chocolates, which to a great extent belong in the province of the professional candy maker and should look precisely turned out, chocolate truffles are supposed to look somewhat rugged. If they looked too neat and evenly rounded, they wouldn't resemble their namesake, the knobby real-life Périgord truffle.

No pig is needed to sniff around in the deep forest of the Périgord long before dawn to find where these truffles grow! All one needs is a small kitchen space, a double boiler, a spoon or two, a baking sheet, and a cold spot in which to let them chill.

In every phase of the culinary arts, flavor is everything, and premium ingredients must be used to achieve the subtle counterpoint of flavors that is possible with the candy recipes given here. The cream and butter must be exquisitely fresh for the sake of "keeping" as well as taste. And the truffles must be refrigerated to stay fresh and firm.

# GRANDMOTHER'S PANTRY

*Hot Artichoke Pickles with Chili Peppers*
*South Carolina Artichoke Pickle*
*Sliced Artichoke Mustard Pickle*
*Jerusalem Artichoke Relish*
*St. James Court Cherry Relish*
*Florida Kumquat Preserves*
*Kumquat Marmalade*
*Apple Preserves with Ginger*
*Black Bing Cherry Preserves*
*Mango and Green Grape Preserves*
*St. Augustine Mincemeat*
*Marvelous Mincemeat*

Some of the happiest memories of my childhood come into focus when I think of my many visits to my grandmother's when I was very young. Grandmother and Grandfather McGregor lived in the country, a short mile from our little town in Kentucky.

Mother was oftentimes too busy to drive me out to Grandmother's, so she would ask J.B. Threlkeld to take me. J.B. lived just a few doors up the street, and he was the proud owner of a Shetland pony named Princess and a cart just barely big enough to hold the two of us. J.B. charged twenty-five cents for the trip. I would pack my tiny valise with a gown and a toothbrush and off we would go. If I decided to spend an extra day or two, it mattered little. J.B. and Princess would come for me on the double, and at no extra cost—the quarter paid for the round-trip.

My grandparents lived in a simple white clapboard house with a white wooden fence whose gate hung loose because of an unscrewed hinge. This gate was a bone of contention, as Grandmother fumed every day over Grandfather's neglect in mending it. But Grandfather was so gentle and sweet, so tall and handsome, I adored him, broken gate or no.

Grandfather attended to the horse and the one cow in the barn and to the two or three hams in the smokehouse. Grandmother raised the chickens and the one "scared" turkey. (For the benefit of city people, turkeys are the neurotics of the barnyard. They are literally scared to death and are a general nuisance to raise, but every farm must have one or two for the holidays.)

I cannot remember who helped with the garden, but I can see it all so clearly. The rhubarb was placed in a back corner—it is an ungainly plant, no matter how delicious. The fresh peas and strawberries were up front. The small orchard to the right of the screechy gate was filled with apple trees, whose fruit I helped gather, but the little black Bing cherry tree in the side yard nearest to the garden was my favorite.

In the late summer and early autumn I would watch Grandmother fill up the shelves in the pantry, called the "cold room," with beautiful vegetables in quart jars and many little glasses of preserves and jellies with their covers of quilting scraps tied to cover the layer of paraffin. "These are for Christmas," Grandmother would say. There were no freezers or electric refrigerators in those days, so the methods of preserving were different, but they worked.

Grandmother always made it a special occasion when I came to visit, and she would have fried country ham and hot biscuits for my breakfast—and, of course, a taste of the latest batch of preserves she'd just made to store in the Christmas pantry.

## HOT ARTICHOKE PICKLES WITH CHILI PEPPERS

In chili peppers, it is the seeds that hold the fire—so to reduce the heat, simply remove some of the seeds.

8 quarts (1 peck) firm Jerusalem artichokes
Pure (uniodized) or pickling salt
1 cup vegetable oil or extra-virgin olive oil
2 teaspoons ground turmeric
4 ounces (1¼ cups) dry mustard
3 pounds sugar
4 quarts (1 gallon) cider vinegar
2 to 4 small hot chili peppers, red or green, fresh or canned
2 or 3 small mild yellow chili peppers
2 tablespoons black peppercorns
4 tablespoons mustard seed
3 tablespoons celery seed

1. Rinse the Jerusalem artichokes and scrub them thoroughly with a very stiff brush. Cut off any soft spots. Place the artichokes in a large kettle and cover them with cold water (measure the water as you add it). Add 2 tablespoons pure or pickling salt for each quart of water. Refrigerate, covered, for 2 or 3 days.
2. Drain the artichokes well and rub them dry with a clean kitchen towel.
3. In a very large mixing bowl, combine the oil, turmeric, and mustard. Beat hard until the mixture is smooth (you can do this in a blender or food processor if you like). Add the sugar and vinegar and mix well.

4. Pour this pickling solution into a large, heavy nonreactive soup pot or kettle. Add the chili peppers, peppercorns, mustard seed, and celery seed. Heat to almost boiling. Remove the pot from the heat and set it aside for 15 to 20 minutes for the flavors to blend; stir the mixture several times.

5. Put the artichokes in large, hot sterilized jars. Bring the pickling solution to a hard boil and pour it over the artichokes, distributing the spices evenly among the jars. Seal and set aside for 6 weeks before using.

Makes 8 quarts

I recommend Colman's—it's the finest dry mustard. One whole can of Colman's weighs 4 ounces.

## South Carolina Artichoke Pickle

My daughter Elissa brought this recipe to me many years ago, when she was in college in South Carolina. Few relishes speak more eloquently of the Deep South's best menus.

8 quarts (1 peck) firm Jerusalem artichokes
Coarse (kosher) or pickling salt
1 small piece alum
1 cup sugar
1 cup dry mustard
4 quarts (1 gallon) cider vinegar
2½ tablespoons celery seed
2 tablespoons whole cloves
1 tablespoon coriander seed
2 tablespoons ground allspice
3½ tablespoons mustard seed

1.  Rinse the Jerusalem artichokes and scrub them thoroughly with a very stiff brush. Cut off any soft spots. Place the artichokes in a large stainless-steel or ceramic bowl or pan and cover them with cold water (measure the water as you add it). Add 1 tablespoon coarse or pickling salt for each quart of water. Cover and refrigerate overnight.
2.  Drain the artichokes. Cover them again with water, stirring in the alum so it dissolves (the alum makes the pickles crisp). Cover and refrigerate overnight.
3.  Drain the artichokes and rinse them thoroughly. Drain them again.
4.  Combine the sugar and mustard in a large saucepan, mixing well. Add the vinegar and all the seeds and spices. Bring to a low boil and cook for 5 minutes. Allow the solution to cool to lukewarm.
5.  Put the artichokes in hot sterilized jars and pour the solution over them, dividing the spices evenly among the jars. Set aside for at least 1 week before serving. Keep covered and refrigerated.

Makes 8 quarts

## SLICED ARTICHOKE MUSTARD PICKLE

All of the Jerusalem artichoke pickle recipes given here will be stars in your pantry and on your table—you'll see!

*3 quarts firm Jerusalem artichokes*
*About 1¼ cups iodized salt*
*1 quart small onions, peeled*
*1 large snow-white cauliflower*
*3 large red bell peppers, or 4 or 5 fresh pimentos*

*3 large green bell peppers*
*1 cup sifted all-purpose flour*
*6 tablespoons dry mustard*
*1 tablespoon ground turmeric*
*4 cups sugar*
*2 quarts cider vinegar*

1. Rinse the Jerusalem artichokes and scrub them thoroughly with a very stiff brush. Cut off any soft spots. Slice the artichokes thin (but not tissue-paper thin). Place the slices in a large stainless-steel or ceramic bowl or pan and cover them with cold water; stir in ¼ cup of the salt. Cover and refrigerate overnight.
2. Slice the onions thin and place them in a bowl. Cover them with cold water and ¼ cup of the salt. Refrigerate or leave in a cool place, covered, overnight.
3. Break the cauliflower into small flowerets. Place them in a bowl and cover with cold water; add ¼ cup of the salt. Refrigerate or leave in a cool place, covered, overnight.
4. Slice the bell peppers very thin and then chop them lightly. Place them in a bowl and cover with cold water; add ¼ cup of the salt. Refrigerate (preferably) or leave in a cool place, covered, overnight.
5. The next day, drain all the vegetables in a colander.
6. In a large, heavy nonreactive saucepan, combine the flour, mustard, turmeric, and a little of the sugar. Mix well. Add some of the vinegar and beat until the mixture forms a smooth paste. Stir in the remaining sugar and vinegar. Bring to a boil and cook, stirring constantly, until the mixture thickens, 6 to 8 minutes. Taste for salt.
7. Add all the vegetables except the artichokes and bring to a hard boil. Then add the artichokes, mixing them in thoroughly. Do not cook the artichokes—remove the pan from the heat.
8. Spoon the vegetables into hot sterilized jars and seal at once. Set them aside for several days to develop their full flavor before serving. Chill the pickle before serving.

Makes 8 to 10 quarts

VARIATION:
If you like, you can chop the vegetables for this pickle. But not too finely, please.

If you're short of bowls or refrigerator space, combine the cauliflower and bell peppers for the overnight soaking (but keep the onions separate).

## JERUSALEM ARTICHOKE RELISH

There are few extra touches to dishes that Southerners enjoy more than relishes of all kinds, and this is one of the best—crunchy, flavorful, and very special.

3 quarts firm Jerusalem artichokes
1 quart sweet onions, peeled
1 large head snow-white cauliflower
6 red bell peppers
2 large green bell peppers
4 quarts water
2 cups coarse (kosher) or pickling salt
6 tablespoons dry mustard
1 tablespoon ground turmeric
1 cup sifted all-purpose flour
4 cups sugar
2 quarts cider vinegar

1. Rinse the Jerusalem artichokes and scrub them thoroughly with a very stiff brush. Cut off any soft spots.

2.  Chop the artichokes and onions and place them in a large ceramic or stainless-steel pan. Break the cauliflower into flowerets and cut them into pieces the size of the artichokes. Seed the bell peppers, chop them, and add them to the other vegetables. Toss the vegetables together to mix them. Cover with the water and salt, cover the pan, and refrigerate for 24 hours.
3.  Drain the vegetables thoroughly.
4.  Combine the mustard, turmeric, flour, and sugar in a large soup pot or kettle, mixing well. Add enough vinegar to form a paste. Then add the rest of the vinegar and bring to a simmer, whisking constantly to keep the flour from forming lumps. Cook until the sauce is thick and smooth, about 15 minutes.
5.  Add the vegetables and bring to a boil. Remove from the heat and immediately spoon into hot sterilized jars. Seal the jars. Let the relish age for a week or more before serving. It will keep on the shelf for months when properly sealed or it can be kept in the refrigerator indefinitely.

Makes 8 to 10 pints

## JERUSALEM ARTICHOKES

The Jerusalem artichoke is a member of the sunflower family—one of its lesser-known members except in gourmet circles and among country-wise people in our Southern states.

The name Jerusalem apparently comes from an Italian word, *girasole*, which means "moving with the sun." It is also called the sunchoke.

The artichoke grows in open spaces, along country roads and in fields, where it can drink in the rays of the sun all summer long. The yellow blooms are smaller than most sunflowers and they grow in groups of three to five on a stem. In the cooler days of late October and November, the flowers and stalks die back, and that is the signal they give to us that their wonderful knobby tubers are ready to be dug and eaten.

I remember quite vividly how each fall when I was a little girl my father would gather the artichokes from a field not far from our home. They are nodular little roots, not at all pretty—they look very much like a knotty potato—but we loved them and ate them with salt, as we did radishes.

John Parkinson (1567–1650), the famous botanist to King Charles I of England, called the artichoke the potato of Canada. Although the flavor of the artichoke is indeed unique, some do think it resembles that of a potato, although ever so faintly. It is as crisp and crunchy as can be and is so delectable eaten raw; in this writer's opinion, it is one of the most neglected vegetables for a crudités platter.

There are a number of ways to cook the Jerusalem artichoke, but its great genius is in relishes and pickles, which Southerners adore, and so does everyone else who is lucky enough to make their acquaintance.

The Jerusalem artichoke relishes are at their best when served with country ham, chicken dishes of every description, turkey, quail, Cornish hen, guinea hen, and duck, and are heaven on earth with pheasant. This talent, above all, makes them most companionable with the traditional winter holiday menus.

## St. James Court Cherry Relish

Great with turkey, ham, or roast beef, this relish also makes a lovely Christmas gift.

*4 pints fresh sour red cherries, stones removed*
*3 cups cider vinegar*
*8 cups sugar*
*Several pieces cinnamon stick (3½ inches each)*

1. Combine the cherries and vinegar in a mixing bowl, cover, and leave overnight in a cool spot or in the refrigerator.
2. The next day, drain the cherries thoroughly and transfer them to a large bowl. Add the sugar and mix well.
3. Cover and refrigerate for 10 days, stirring them once a day.
4. Spoon the cherries into hot sterilized jars. Add a cinnamon stick to each jar and seal. Set aside for at least 1 month before serving.

Makes 4 pints

## FLORIDA KUMQUAT PRESERVES

Late November and early December is the time to make these old-fashioned preserves, a Christmas favorite.

4 pounds perfect kumquats
1 teaspoon baking soda
4 cups sugar
4 cups water
1 slice lemon

1. Rinse the kumquats and scrub them thoroughly. Place them in a large bowl, sprinkle the baking soda over them, and cover with boiling water. Set aside for 10 to 12 minutes.
2. Drain the kumquats, rinse them in cold water, and drain again. Using a sharp knife, make four slits in each kumquat. Place them in a large saucepan, cover with cold water, and cook at a medium boil for 15 minutes.
3. Drain the kumquats and cover them again with cold water. Boil until tender, about 5 minutes.
4. Meanwhile, combine the sugar and water in a large saucepan and bring to a boil; cook for 5 minutes and then set aside to cool completely.

5. Drain the kumquats and add them to the cooled sugar syrup along with the lemon slice. Bring to a boil again and cook until the fruit is clear, about 10 minutes. Cover and refrigerate overnight or as long as 24 hours.
6. Bring the kumquats and syrup to a low boil. Remove from the heat and spoon into hot sterilized jars, discarding the lemon slice if you like. Seal at once. Let the preserves age for a week or longer before serving.

Makes 2 pints

## KUMQUAT MARMALADE

Winter is kumquat season, so this marmalade is a special holiday treat.

*24 perfect kumquats, as small as possible*
*1 teaspoon baking soda*
*2 or 3 navel oranges*
*Sugar*
*6 tablespoons fresh lemon juice*

1. Rinse the kumquats and scrub them thoroughly. Place them in a bowl, sprinkle the baking soda over them, and cover with boiling water. Set aside for 10 minutes.
2. Drain the kumquats, rinse them, and slice them paper-thin. Discard the seeds.
3. Juice the oranges (you need ⅔ cup juice). Chop the orange peel and pulp in a food processor.
4. In a large saucepan, combine the kumquats, orange juice, and orange peel and pulp. Measure the quantity of fruit and add 3 cups water for each cup of fruit. Allow to stand in a cool place for 18 hours or overnight.
5. Bring the fruit mixture to a boil and simmer until the orange peel is tender, 10 to 15 minutes.

6. Measure the amount of fruit and liquid and add ¾ cup sugar for each cup of fruit mixture. Stir in the lemon juice. Bring to a medium boil and cook until the marmalade reaches the jellying point, 222°F to 224°F. Remove the pan from the heat.

7. Spoon the marmalade into hot sterilized jelly glasses and seal with melted paraffin, or you can refrigerate or freeze the cooled marmalade.

Makes 2 to 3 cups

### KUMQUATS

The kumquat is not considered by biologists to be a true citrus fruit. It is native to southeastern China and is cultivated in the United States mostly in Florida and California. The fruit is found in our markets only at the height of winter and is especially enjoyed at the Christmas season. In China it is a treasured custom during the holidays to give kumquat trees as gifts.

In Western countries in days gone by, when kumquats were a greater novelty, it was a custom to place small kumquat trees on the table at a fashionable dinner. Each guest would pick a kumquat to accompany dessert and demitasse.

## APPLE PRESERVES WITH GINGER

This is one of the finest of all apple preserves—great for turnovers, cookie filling, fruitcakes, and puddings.

3 pounds firm tart apples, such as Winesap, Granny Smith,
    Yellow Delicious, or Rome
2½ cups cold water
3 cups sugar
2 teaspoons fresh lemon juice, or to taste
2 slices crystallized or preserved ginger, slivered

1.  Wash, core, and peel the apples. Cut them into eighths. You should have
    about 2 pounds of prepared apples.
2.  Combine the water and sugar in a large saucepan and bring to a boil. Boil
    for 2½ to 3 minutes. Set aside to cool.
3.  Stir the apples, lemon juice, and ginger into the cooled sugar syrup. Bring
    to a boil and cook gently until the apples are clear and transparent. You
    want to keep the apples intact, so cook them gently and shake the pan
    instead of stirring the mixture.
4.  Remove the pan from the heat and using a sterilized slatted spoon, transfer
    the apples to hot sterilized jars, leaving a ½-inch headspace.
5.  Bring the syrup back to a boil and cook almost to the jellying point, 118°F
    to 120°F. Spoon the syrup over the apples, leaving a ½-inch headspace.
    Allow the preserves to cool, then cover and refrigerate. They will keep
    indefinitely.

Makes about 2 pints

## BLACK BING CHERRY PRESERVES

With a cherry pitter such as the German one made by
Westmann-Kerner, these preserves are a song to make. Bing
cherries do not have much pectin, but lemons do, so these preserves gel
nicely.

5 cups Bing cherries, pitted
2 cups sugar
½ cup water
⅓ cup fresh lemon juice

1. Combine the cherries and sugar in a heavy, shallow nonreactive pan. Set them aside to plump, several hours or as long as overnight.
2. Add the water to the cherries and bring to a boil. Cook for 5 minutes. Then add the lemon juice and boil rather fast until the juice has thickened like jelly and a candy thermometer reads 221°F. Remove the pan from the heat and allow the preserves to sit overnight, covered; refrigerate them if you like.
3. The next day, reheat the preserves to boiling and then spoon them into hot sterilized jars and seal. You can also store them in the refrigerator or (better) in the freezer.

Makes 1½ pints

## MANGO AND GREEN GRAPE PRESERVES

This is a Lucullan preserve. It is delicious with hot rolls, hot biscuits, or with cream cheese on crisp crackers. Try it also with goat cheese or sour cream pancakes, with a butter kuchen, or with a delicious pound cake.

3 pounds green seedless grapes, preferably small Thompson grapes
3 or 4 very large unripe mangoes
2½ to 3 pounds sugar
1 cup cider vinegar
½ cup water
3 cinnamon sticks (3½ inches long), broken into thirds
1 tablespoon whole cloves
4 thin slices lemon
½ cup preserved or crystallized ginger, slivered

1. Cut the grapes in half lengthwise.
2. Peel the mangoes and cut them into very large slices (you should have 3 pounds). Pour 1 cup of the sugar over the mangoes, cover them, and set them aside in a cool place for several hours or as long as overnight.
3. Combine the remaining sugar, the vinegar, and the water in a heavy non-reactive pan. Add the cinnamon sticks, cloves, lemon, and ginger. Bring to a boil, stirring to dissolve the sugar, and cook for about 3 minutes.
4. Add the mangoes to the syrup and boil gently for about 15 minutes. Then add the grapes and simmer until the mango slices are just tender when pierced with a cooking fork, 15 to 20 minutes.
5. Using a slatted spoon, fill hot sterilized jars ¾ full with the preserves. If the syrup is not as thick as corn syrup, boil it until it reaches 222°F on a candy thermometer. Pour the hot syrup over the fruit, leaving a ½-inch head-space. Seal at once.

Makes about 4½ pints

VARIATION:
You can make this recipe with peaches or nectarines, but the mango makes a far superior preserve.

Part of the sugar is added to the mangoes ahead of time so they will absorb the sugar.

## ST. AUGUSTINE MINCEMEAT

This mincemeat is deliciously different and very versatile—a real discovery for your Christmas collection.

1½ cups chopped peeled apples
1½ cups chopped peeled unripe pears
1 cup sultana (golden) raisins
½ cup dried currants

¼ cup bitter orange marmalade
1 cup sugar, or to taste
2 teaspoons ground cinnamon
1 teaspoon ground cloves
1 tablespoon preserved or crystallized ginger, slivered
½ cup chopped blanched almonds or walnuts
½ teaspoon salt, or to taste
3 tablespoons Cointreau, or 1 tablespoon rum, cognac, or aged bourbon

1. Combine all the ingredients except the Cointreau in a heavy saucepan (not aluminum). Bring to a boil and cook over a medium heat until the mixture is well flavored and the apples are tender, about 40 minutes. Taste for sweetness and add sugar if necessary.
2. Remove the pan from the heat and stir in the Cointreau (this is my choice of liqueur because it blends so well with the orange marmalade). Spoon the mincemeat into hot sterilized jars. It will keep indefinitely in the refrigerator without sealing (but do cover it).

Makes about 2 pints

VARIATION:
You can substitute peach or apricot preserves for the orange marmalade.

## MARVELOUS MINCEMEAT

Mincemeat is at its best when made ahead and allowed to ripen for several weeks. The ginger in this recipe is especially tangy and unusual; you can omit it if you like . . . but please don't!

½ pound beef kidney suet, ground
2 cups sticky raisins (seeded, not Thompson)
2 cups dried currants
4 cups chopped peeled apples

*1 or 2 guavas, peeled and chopped (optional)*
*1 cup sugar*
*½ cup finely chopped glazed citron*
*½ cup finely chopped candied lemon peel*
*½ cup finely chopped candied orange peel*
*2 tablespoons chopped crystallized or preserved ginger*
*1½ teaspoons ground cinnamon*
*1 teaspoon freshly grated nutmeg*
*½ teaspoon ground cloves*
*1 teaspoon ground allspice*
*2 teaspoons coarse (kosher) or sea salt*
*1 cup brandy or bourbon, plus extra as needed*

1.  Combine all the ingredients except the brandy in a large mixing bowl and toss well to mix. Stir in the 1 cup brandy. Spoon the mincemeat mixture into a ceramic, stainless-steel, or plastic container with a cover and pour a little extra brandy over the top.
2.  Cover tightly and store in the refrigerator or a very cool place for 3 to 6 weeks. (If you do not store it in the refrigerator, make sure the mixture is well covered with liquid.)

Makes about 6 pints

Ask your butcher to give you kidney suet; it is the least fibrous suet.

# INDEX